Difficult Questions for Christians

Steve Gravett

O&U
Onwards & Upwards

Difficult Questions for Christians

Onwards and Upwards Publishers
3 Radfords Turf, Cranbrook, Exeter,
EX5 7DX, United Kingdom.
www.onwardsandupwards.org

Copyright © Steve Gravett 2019

The right of Steve Gravett to be identified as the author of this work has been asserted by the author in accordance with the Copyright, Designs and Patents Act 1988.

All rights reserved.

No part of this publication may be reproduced or transmitted in any form or by any means, electronic or mechanical, including photocopy, recording or any information storage and retrieval system, without permission in writing from the author or publisher.

First edition, published in the United Kingdom by Onwards and Upwards Publishers (2019).

ISBN:	978-1-78815-560-1
Typeface:	Sabon LT
Graphic design:	LM Graphic Design

The views and opinions expressed in this book are the author's own, and do not necessarily represent the views and opinions of Onwards and Upwards Publishers or its staff

---

Scripture quotations marked (AMP) are taken from the Amplified® Bible, Copyright © 2015 by The Lockman Foundation. Used by permission. www.Lockman.org Scripture quotations marked (ESV) are from the ESV® Bible (The Holy Bible, English Standard Version®), copyright © 2001 by Crossway, a publishing ministry of Good News Publishers. Used by permission. All rights reserved. Scripture quotations marked (MSG) are taken from THE MESSAGE. Copyright © by Eugene H. Peterson 1993, 1994, 1995, 1996, 2000, 2001, 2002. Used by permission of NavPress. All rights reserved. Represented by Tyndale House Publishers, Inc. Scripture quotations marked (NIV) are taken from THE HOLY BIBLE, NEW INTERNATIONAL VERSION®, NIV® Copyright © 1973, 1978, 1984, 2011 by Biblica, Inc.™ Used by permission. All rights reserved worldwide. Scripture quotations marked (NKJV) are taken from the New King James Version®. Copyright © 1982 by Thomas Nelson. Used by permission. All rights reserved. Scripture quotations marked (NLT) are taken from the Holy Bible, New Living Translation, copyright © 1996, 2004, 2007, 2013 by Tyndale House Foundation. Used by permission of Tyndale House Publishers, Inc., Carol Stream, Illinois 60188. All rights reserved. Scripture quotations marked (NRSV) are from the New Revised Standard Version Bible, copyright © 1989 National Council of the Churches of Christ in the United States of America. Used by permission. All rights reserved.

Endorsements

Christmas, gay marriage, predestination, mercy killing, angels and so much more is covered in this illuminating and challenging book. Fascinating, informative and inspiring – I commend this book for Christians of all ages and all denominations.

Dr. Barrie Lawrence
Chairman of National Council,
Full Gospel Businessmen UK & Ireland

Difficult Question for Christians sets out biblical teaching on a number of current questions that would be particularly appropriate for a new Christian, and also that would help to dispel the fog of ignorance and indifference that sadly darkens many people's minds these days.

The Reverend Canon Bernard Baker
Retired minister, St James Church, Ryde, Isle of Wight

About the Author

Steve Gravett was adopted by godly Christian parents as a baby. He accepted Jesus Christ as his personal Saviour at the age of six and has been a committed practising Christian ever since. Steve has been involved in church ministry in a variety of leadership roles with children, young people and adults. He and his wife attend Grace Church in Ryde, on the Isle of Wight. He is a member of the Full Gospel Businessmen and the Gideons.

Steve is a trained social worker and joined Her Majesty's Prison Service, where he trained for two years as an Assistant Governor until promoted to the role of Prison Governor. Over a period of four years he wrote a regular column for *Community Care* and published four professional books.

To contact the author, please visit his website:

www.steveauthor.co.uk

or send an email to:

stevegravett2@gmail.com

More information about the author can also be found on the book's web page:

www.onwardsandupwards.org/difficult-questions-for-christians

Acknowledgements

Thanks and appreciation to the following:

- Jonathan Snell, Assemblies of God Minister at Sandown (retired), for the foreword and his spiritual insights, suggestions and encouragement.
- Full Gospel Businessmen UK & Ireland for the postscript.
- My son, Jonathan Gravett, for designing the website *www.steveauthor.co.uk*.

Difficult Questions for Christians

Dedication

To Beryl, my patient and supportive wife,

our three inspiring children,
Jonathan, Joy and Faye,

Simon, our much-loved son-in-law,

and our beautiful grandchildren, Zachary, Ava, Laylee, Kai, Harry and Poppy.

Difficult Questions for Christians

Contents

Preface 13
Foreword by Jonathan Snell 15
Key to Translations 16

1. Why Is God So Intolerant? 17
2. Christening, Dedication or Baptism? 30
3. Celebrating the Last Supper 44
4. Are Christians Really Any Different? 58
5. Are Spiritual Gifts Relevant Today? 73
6. Should I Tithe if I Pay Tax? 89
7. Why is Predestination Such a Dilemma? 98
8. Can God Bless Gay Marriages? 108
9. Should Mercy-Killing Be Made Legal? 118
10. Are Angels Real? 132
11. Why do Christians Celebrate Pagan Festivals? 150

Postscript: How Can I Become a Christian? 164
Bibliography 165

Difficult Questions for Christians

"All scripture is inspired by God and is useful for teaching, for reproof, for correction, and for training in righteousness."

2 Timothy 3:16 (NRSV)

"I believe the Bible to be the inspired, the only infallible, authoritative Word of God."

Steve Gravett

Difficult Questions for Christians

Preface

This book recognises there are many difficult questions to answer about Christianity, even for those who have been believers for many years.

Sometimes church practices are confusing, like infant baptism or transubstantiation, other times it is knowing how best to live a Christian life. Understanding teaching on difficult issues like the gifts of the Holy Spirit is challenging, as is knowing how a Christian should think on issues like mercy-killing and gay marriage; topics that are exercising the minds of some theologians. Nobody has all the answers, but the Bible gives clear guidance on many difficult questions we face today.

This book examines eleven of the more difficult questions Christians face, employing a user-friendly approach that places great emphasis on what the Bible teaches. It draws on seven modern translations and a number of commentaries, in order to ensure clarity and scriptural accuracy. Every statement is supported by a supporting quotation from the Bible, reproduced in full, to save the reader from having to spend time searching the scriptures for themselves.

The format of the book is designed to inform and encourage debate and discussion. This approach makes it suitable for use in church, in a small group, in the classroom, in a residential home or in a penal establishment. It will help Christians have a biblical view on all these contemporary issues tackled and equip them to "always be prepared to give an answer to everyone who asks you to give the reason for the hope that you have"[1].

This book also caters for the reader who has not yet made a decision to become a Christian but is seeking to know more and is wondering whether Christianity has the answers. Be encouraged to persevere; nobody knows all the answers. The postscript is designed for seekers who wish to accept Jesus Christ as their personal Saviour. It shows you how to become a Christian and contains three steps and a simple prayer of salvation.

---

[1] 1 Peter 3:15 (NIV)

Difficult Questions for Christians

The author believes the Bible has the answers to all of life's questions and challenges, as it contains wisdom, insight, spiritual guidance and reveals life lessons if approached thoughtfully and in a spirit of humility.

Pray that God will give you insight as you study his word and that this book will encourage you to keep on asking questions.

If you have any comments you would like to make or have a question about anything you have read, please feel free to contact me by email at *stevegravett2@gmail.com*.

Further information can be obtained by contacting my website:

www.steveauthor.co.uk

Foreword by Jonathan Snell

The following pages of this book will be an interesting and stimulating read for all Christians who enjoy thinking about their faith. Steve is not afraid to tackle difficult issues and deal with some controversial questions robustly. He does so with shrewdness and typical thoroughness while remaining anchored in scripture. His broad and varied experience of life as a social work team leader and a prison governor enables him to take a balanced view of Christian sacraments and practice, as does his awareness of different denominational viewpoints.

I recommend the author to you, the reader, knowing him not only as a good-humoured, honest and lively, insightful friend, but as an efficient, straightforward church trustee with a passion for accuracy and integrity during my pastoral ministry.

Steve has a real desire to minister to people through his writing. Topics he has chosen will be very relevant to parents and all those involved in helping others in the church and society of today. I believe his book will be a blessing to you.

Jonathan Snell
Retired Assemblies of God Minister

Key to Translations

AMP	Amplified Bible
ESV	English Standard Version
MSG	The Message
NIV	New International Version
NKJV	New King James Version
NLT	New Living Translation
NRSV	New Revised Standard Version

Chapter One

Why Is God So Intolerant?

Introduction

There has to be zero tolerance when dealing with precision engineering, scientific matters, space exploration, financial matters, mathematics, technological innovation and information technology, otherwise we would be living in chaos.

On the other hand, as a society we have become increasingly more tolerant, considering ourselves to be liberal and broadminded to the point we are prepared to compromise on important moral issues under the guise of 'live and let live'.

On one hand we tolerate divorce, adultery, immorality, abortion, drugs and alcohol misuse, corruption, greed in business and government, delinquency and criminal behaviour, such as speeding, drunkenness and insurance fraud. On the other hand, we are intolerant of homophobia, misogyny, political incorrectness and, increasingly, Christianity.

There is a view 'all roads lead to heaven'. This mistaken belief is based on the assumption that if an individual attends church occasionally, or tries to be a good person by leading a decent life or being generous to the poor or supporting charities and Food Banks, God will overlook their shortcomings and they will go to heaven.

There is plenty of evidence that Jesus loved sinners and went around doing good, healing the sick and preaching about the Kingdom of heaven because he was not willing for anybody to go to a lost eternity in hell. However, Jesus had no time for hypocrites who misled others, or arrogant and selfish people, and said as much during his preaching ministry.

When we unpack what is meant by being tolerant it is generally understood to mean a liberal, open-minded person who condones the opinions and behaviour of others, even though they do not necessarily agree with them.

However, God has 'zero tolerance' with sin and is unwilling to compromise his standards or accept any deviation from his commandments as set out in the Bible.

When Billy Graham was asked, "What is the definition of sin?" he gave the following answer: "A sin is any thought or action that falls short of God's will. God is perfect, and anything we do that falls short of his perfection is sin."[2]

> *All have sinned and continually fall short of the glory of God.*
>
> Romans 3:23 (AMP)

The apostle Paul was unequivocal.

> *For the wages of sin is death, but the free gift of God (that is, His remarkable gift of grace to believers) is eternal life in Christ Jesus our Lord.*
>
> Romans 6:23 (AMP)

Jesus and Hypocrites

The word 'hypocrite' is derived from the Greek term for 'actor' – literally 'one who wears a mask'. Hypocrisy can take two forms: those who profess to believe something but act in a manner that is contrary to that belief, or someone who looks down on others when they have similar shortcomings to themselves but which they conveniently ignore.

Jesus was critical of the Pharisees, who were the religious leaders of the day, because they did not practise what they preached. They were proud, self-centred, insincere leaders of the synagogue, who enjoyed the status of being called 'Rabbi', but lacked the humility, compassion and kindness that are the mark of great leaders.

They were keen to ensure the minute detail of the law of Moses was religiously followed by ordinary Jews, and were quick to judge others and point out any of their shortcomings.

Jesus says, 'Woe to you, teachers of the law and Pharisees, you hypocrites!'[3] and goes on to describe them as 'blind guides'[4] and 'blind

---

[2] *www.billygraham.org*
[3] Matthew 23:15 (NIV)
[4] Matthew 23:16 (NIV)

fools'[5]. Jesus makes pointed remarks about the hypocrisy of the Pharisees, using the amusing metaphor of a person with a plank in their eye trying to see a piece of sawdust in someone else's eye!

> *"How can you say to your brothers, 'Let me take the speck out of your eye,' while all the time there is a plank in your own eye? You hypocrite, first take the plank out of your own eye, and then you will see clearly to remove the speck from your brother's eye."*
>
> *Matthew 7:4-5 (NIV)*

The lesson here is to ensure our lives are above reproach and we correct our shortcomings before we have the temerity to criticize others.

Jesus compares the Scribes and Pharisees to false prophets and teachers, who appear to be placid like sheep, but in reality are ferocious wolves. He also uses the analogy of good and bad fruit, pointing out a bad or diseased tree cannot bear good fruit, so ultimately the bad tree has to be cut down and destroyed by fire. The apostle Paul says we can recognize good fruit when we see the evidence of the nine 'fruit of the Spirit' in a believer's life.[6]

The problem with the Scribes and Pharisees was everything they did was for show; none of it was genuine as their sole aim was to make themselves look virtuous. Jesus could not tolerate their hypocrisy and forcefully condemned it.

> *"You're hopeless, you religion scholars and Pharisees! Frauds! You're like manicured grave plots, grass clipped and the flowers bright, but six feet down it's all rotting bones and worm-eaten flesh. People look at you and think you're saints, but beneath the skin you're total frauds."*
>
> *Matthew 23:27-28 (MSG)*

Jesus had 'zero tolerance' with the religious leaders and their hypocritical behaviour and could deliver a scathing put-down. It is no wonder he was so popular with the people but was hated by the religious leaders of the day.

---

[5] Matthew 23:17 (NIV)
[6] See Galatians 5:22

Jesus Desires Humility

Jesus told a parable about two men at the temple. The first was a Pharisee who selected a prominent position to pray where everybody could see how virtuous he was.

> "'God, I thank you that I am not like other people – robbers, evildoers, adulterers – or even like this tax collector. I fast twice a week and give a tenth of all I get.'"
>
> Luke 18:11-12 (NIV)

Compare this self-righteous and arrogant attitude with the demeanour of the tax collector who stood where he could not be seen and was so distressed by his sinfulness that he averted his eyes from heaven.

> "'God, have mercy on me, a sinner.'"
>
> Luke 18:14 (NIV)

Jesus made it clear that the unpopular tax collector was the one who went home 'justified before God'[7] because he displayed humility before God and was truly repentant.

When Jesus gave the Sermon on the Mount, part of which is known as the Beatitudes, he made it clear humility was a virtue that brought with it a blessing.

> "Blessed (spiritually prosperous, happy, to be admired) are the poor in spirit [those devoid of spiritual arrogance, or those who regard themselves as insignificant], for theirs is the kingdom of heaven (both now and forever)."
>
> Matthew 5:3 (AMP)

Jesus Challenges Sin

God does not care about being tolerant, he cares about truth! There is a modern tendency to deny the reality of sin by sanitizing it and calling it something else. An example of this denial is the notion of 'friends with benefits', a euphemism for a casual sexual relationship which the Bible condemns as fornication.

Another example is when an individual fraudulently inflates the scale of their car or home insurance losses and justifies their dishonesty by

---

[7] Luke 18:14 (NIV)

calling it a 'victimless crime'. We all know this is untrue. The cost of this fraudulent action is inflated premiums for every other policy-holder.

> *(Judgment is coming) to those who call evil good, and good evil.*
>
> Isaiah 5:20 (AMP)

The Scribes and Pharisees brought a woman to Jesus who had been caught red-handed in the act of adultery, and asked Jesus to tell them what they should do. Jesus recognized this was an attempt to trap him, given the Mosaic law decreed stoning was the appropriate punishment for both parties found in an adulterous relationship. They knew Jesus would not sanction having her put to death. It was also misogyny, as they allowed the man found to be consorting with her to go free, which was contrary to Mosaic law!

> *If a man is found sleeping with another man's wife, both the man who slept with her and the woman must die.*
>
> Deuteronomy 22:22 (NIV)

The legal position was not straightforward, partly because the man responsible was not produced. Some scholars believe the woman concerned was Mary Magdalene who was possessed (and later healed of possessing) seven demons,[8] which would have been considered mitigation. During the period of the rabbinic law, the Mosaic punishments were substantially modified and additional requirements for securing a conviction were added, so a full trial would have been necessary. Jesus discerned the deceitful motives and double standards of the religious leaders and wisely refused to answer directly.

> *'Let anyone of you who is without sin be the first to throw a stone at her.'*
>
> John 8:7 (NIV)

The outcome was that they all slowly disappeared, as no one was willing to take responsibility for throwing the first stone; so eventually Jesus and the woman were left alone. Jesus showed his compassion for the adulterous woman (as opposed to the sin of adultery) and assured her he did not condemn her either.

---

[8] See Luke 8:2

> *Jesus said, "Neither do I condemn you; go, and from now on sin no more."*
>
> John 8:11 (ESV)

On another occasion Jesus went up to Jerusalem for the Jewish Passover. He was filled with righteous indignation as he discovered the temple courts were full of money changers and traders selling animals for sacrifices.

Jesus displayed considerable courage as he made a whip, which was a symbol of prophetic authority,[9] then single-handedly drove out all the animals and doves from the temple, before overturning the money changers' tables and driving them out too.

> *"Get these out of here! Stop turning my Father's house into a market!"*
>
> John 2:16 (NIV)

Jesus was aware the money changers and traders were exploiting the poor as they had to convert their money to the 'Jewish shekel'[10] in order to pay the atonement tax and purchase animals for sacrifice. Jesus had no time for the greedy, selfish traders who exploited the poor and acted dishonestly, and he made his feelings known before allegorically prophesying his death and resurrection.

God's Intolerance of Sin

G. K. Chesterton, a twentieth century philosopher and writer, said, 'Tolerance is the virtue of the man without convictions.' In our politically correct society, it is expected that we accept without question everything about another person's race, religion, sexual orientation, lifestyle and opinions.

Christians can be guilty of following this trend by making the mistake of accepting society's values as the prevailing standard, without applying biblical standards and exercising good judgment.

The Bible teaches how to identify a true Christian by the unselfish way they live their life.

---

[9] See 1 Kings 12:14-15
[10] See Exodus 30:15

Why Is God So Intolerant?

> *But the fruit of the Spirit is love, joy, peace, patience, kindness, goodness, faithfulness, gentleness and self-control...*
>
> *Galatians 5:22-23 (ESV)*

Notice that 'tolerance' is not part of that list – because Christians are not called to be tolerant as they serve a God who has 'zero tolerance' with sin. The Bible talks of the 'acts of the flesh', which are the impulses we choose to act upon because we lack self-control; we are basically wicked, selfish individuals when dominated by our old nature.

> *The acts of the flesh are obvious: sexual immorality, impurity and debauchery; idolatry and witchcraft; hatred, discord, jealousy, fits of rage, selfish ambition, dissentions, factions and envy; drunkenness, orgies, and the like. I warn you, as I did before, that those who live like this will not inherit the kingdom of God.*
>
> *Galatians 5:19-22 (NIV)*

Paul's warning is clear; nobody who acts like this will be going to heaven; they are destined for eternal separation from God for all eternity, unless they repent of their sins and accept Jesus Christ as their Lord and Saviour.

If we examine the position logically from God's viewpoint, only God is by definition good. If good tolerates evil, it ceases to be good. It follows therefore that God cannot tolerate evil; it has to be dealt with and that involves judgment and punishment.

Consider the following three examples of God's intolerance of sin.

In the Garden of Eden, Adam and Eve enjoyed a perfect state of fellowship with God which was designed to last for eternity. The act of eating from the tree of the knowledge of good and evil meant they brought sin into the world, which was not part of God's plan. The punishment for this fragrant disobedience was banishment from the Garden of Eden forever. The human race has paid the price for the introduction of sin into the world ever since. The consequence of sin is separation from God, death, suffering, wearisome labour and the pain of childbirth. Our sin has led to world wars and all around us we see evidence of cruelty, abuse, greed and the exploitation of the weakest members of society. On an individual level, dissatisfaction and guilt can be attributed to pursuing the gods of materialism and power, in contravention of God's laws.

Difficult Questions for Christians

The second example concerns Noah and the flood. 'The earth was corrupt in God's sight and full of violence'[11] so God decided to destroy everybody, except Noah and his family who were godly and faithful people. He sent catastrophic judgment in the form of 'rain on the earth for forty days and forty nights'[12] which caused the biggest flood the world had ever known and 'covered the mountains to a depth of more than fifteen cubits'[13].

The third example of God's 'zero tolerance' of sin concerns the judgment God visited on the cities of Sodom and Gomorrah. They had become exceedingly wicked and immoral so God annihilated them completely. '...the LORD rained down burning sulphur on Sodom and Gomorrah – from the LORD out of the heavens'[14] which killed all those living in the cities and burned up all the vegetation in the land. The following morning all that could be seen was dense smoke rising up from the land like smoke from a furnace. The only people spared were the godly, law-abiding Lot and his two daughters, who made it safely to the town of Zoar. Even Lot's wife died; she was turned into a pillar of salt, because she disobeyed God and 'looked back' when fleeing the city.

What the Bible Teaches About Salvation

Tolerance is not a virtue; repentance is! *Metania* is the Greek word for 'repentance' and implies making a decision to turn around, to face a new direction and have a complete change of heart. Matthew records how Jesus began his Galilean ministry after learning that John the Baptist had been put in prison.

> *From that time Jesus began to preach and to say, "Repent for the kingdom of heaven is at hand."*
>
> Matthew 4:17 (NKJV)

Both the Old and New Testaments show how God has 'zero tolerance' of sin. God provides a way of escaping judgment through redemptive love; that is, God's sacrificial love for mankind, which he demonstrated by sending his Son to pay the price of sin by dying for the sins of all mankind.

---

[11] Genesis 6:11 (ESV)
[12] Genesis 7:4 (NIV)
[13] Genesis 7:20 (NIV); a cubit equals eighteen inches
[14] Genesis 19:24 (NIV)

Jesus was intolerant of anyone who thought and taught there were other ways to reach heaven, such as living a law-abiding life or giving generously to the poor.

> *"For wide is the gate and broad that leads to destruction and many enter through it. But small is the gate and narrow the road that leads to life and only a few find it."*
>
> Matthew 7:13-14 (NIV)
>
> *"I am the way and the truth and the life. No one comes to the Father except through me."*
>
> John 14: 6 (NIV)

There is no other way for us to become acceptable to God except by accepting Jesus as our personal Saviour. There is no wiggle room. No room for compromise or discussion, as the rich young ruler found when he asked Jesus, 'What good thing must I do to get eternal life?'[15]

Jesus' reply was unpalatable, but not surprising, given the rich man thought he could obtain his salvation with his riches, without changing his selfish priorities.

> *"If you want to be perfect, go, sell your possessions and give to the poor, and you will have treasure in heaven. Then come and follow me." When the young man heard this, he went away sad, because he had great wealth.*
>
> Matthew 19:21–22 (NIV)
>
> *It wasn't the giving of his goods that Jesus demanded, but his release from selfishness and its devastating effect on his personality and life.*[16]
>
> Billy Graham

There is only one way that a person can decontaminate their soul from sin and that is to believe Jesus has paid the price once and for all by dying on the cross for their sins. Once Jesus becomes your Saviour or Deliverer, which is *soter* in the Greek, you become 'born again' into a new life and become a Christian. You receive the assurance that your sins

---

[15] Matthew 19:16 (NIV)
[16] Billy Graham; *The Sin of Intolerance;* Billy Graham Evangelistic Association (28/11/2006)

Difficult Questions for Christians

are not only forgiven but forgotten, and can rely on God's promise of eternal life with him in heaven.

> *For God did not send his Son into the world to condemn the world, but to save the world through him.*
>
> John 3:17 (NIV)

Points for Reflection

God in his grace and mercy decided to send his son Jesus Christ to die on the cross in our place because he has zero tolerance of sin. The Bible says everybody who refuses to believe in him or ignores him will be lost eternally. Billy Graham would make this appeal: 'Come to Christ today, while his Spirit is speaking to your heart!'

> *For the wages of sin is death, but the gift of eternal life, in Christ Jesus our Lord.*
>
> Romans 6:23 (NIV)

Paul, writing to the church in Thessalonica, encourages them to remain faithful despite suffering severe persecution and experiencing injustice. He tells them God will avenge those who persecute Christians and reminds them there are only two destinies facing everybody: either to be with God for ever, or to spend eternity in hell.

> *[Jesus] will punish those who do not know God and do not obey the gospel of our Lord Jesus. They will be punished with everlasting destruction and shut out from the presence of the Lord and from the glory of his might on the day he comes to be glorified in his holy people.*
>
> 2 Thessalonians 1:8-10 (NIV)

The Greek word for 'church' is *ekklesia* which means 'called out ones' and refers to all those who meet together as believers; we are the church. Paul reminds us of the need to act like God's chosen people and display the qualities of 'compassion, kindness, humility, gentleness, and patience'[17]. We are to forgive one another as the Lord forgave us, to live in love and to 'let the peace of Christ rule in our hearts'[18].

---

[17] Colossians 3:12 (NIV)
[18] Colossians 3:15 (NIV)

In the meantime his church are warned to be careful about false teaching and divisions appearing in the church amongst God's people. We must not forget that whilst we are believers, there is still an ongoing conflict between good and evil. Christians need to be on their guard against those who want to disrupt the unity of the church. Paul advises that the best way to prevent this happening is to be 'completely humble and gentle; be patient, bearing with one another in love'[19].

> *Watch out for those who cause divisions and put obstacles in your way that are contrary to the teaching you have learned. Keep away from them. For such people are not serving our Lord Christ, but their own appetites. By smooth talk and flattery they deceive the minds of naïve people.*
>
> Romans 16:17-18 (NIV)

A Personal Challenge

The challenge for each believer is not to be afraid to speak out. The world is full of people who are heading for a lost eternity without Christ. We need to be faithful and remember that Jesus said, 'No one can serve two masters.'[20]

Shortly before Joshua died at the age of one hundred and ten, he reminded all the tribes of Israel, its leaders and judges, of the timeless faithfulness of God who brought them safely out of Egypt and into the promised land. God saved them from being made slaves by the Amorites, the Perizzites, the Canaanites, the Hittites, the Hivites, the Girgashites and the Jebusites. In spite of all the blessings they had received, they persisted in worshipping other gods, so Joshua laid down the law to them in the following terms.

> *"You are not able to serve the LORD. He is a holy God; he is a jealous God. He will not forgive your rebellion and your sins. If you forsake the LORD and serve foreign gods, he will turn and bring disaster on you and make an end of you, after he has been good to you."*
>
> Joshua 24:19-20 (NIV)

---

[19] Ephesians 4:2 (NIV)
[20] Matthew 6:24 (NIV)

He challenged them to choose which God they were prepared to serve faithfully, and that challenge is still as relevant today. We all need to make an unreserved commitment and unashamedly say, 'As for me and my house, we will serve the Lord.'[21]

If you are not yet a believer and have been challenged by these scriptures, please turn to the postscript. There you can follow the three steps outlined, which show you how to become a Christian.

---

[21] Joshua 24:15 (ESV)

Questions

How can God be good and tolerate evil?

Why does God not intervene to stop the terrible evil that is widespread in the world today?

Should Christians seek to counsel other believers about their sins and shortcomings?

Are we responsible for our children's sinful behaviour given they were, like us all, born sinful?

How do Christians prevent a lack of unity amongst believers in the church?

How can we encourage new Christians in the church to grow in maturity?

Chapter Two

Christening, Dedication or Baptism?

Introduction

Although most churches practise baptism, the theology and practice varies in different denominations. Churches have argued for centuries whether the Bible supports infant baptism or purely the baptism of believers. Baptism represents the death, burial and resurrection of Jesus Christ and this explains why the Greek word *baptizo* is always used, because it means 'immersion'.

Over the centuries, different denominations of the established church have incorporated many different ideas into their worship to encourage engagement by the congregation of a church. This examination will consider the most common contemporary church practices, including christening, dedication, infant baptism and full immersion in water baptism. The Bible is the only objective way to discover what is truth, so we will evaluate current practice and judge it according to what the scriptures mean by baptism.

Christening

First, we will examine the subject of christening. The Greek word for sprinkling is *rhantizo* and the Greek word *proschusis* means 'pouring or sprinkling on something or someone'. Christening is a ceremony where a baby is named and welcomed into the church. During the ceremony of christening, water is sprinkled or poured over the head of the baby. Alternatively, the baby is immersed in water for a second or two.

The ceremony of christening is usually referred to as 'infant baptism'. Many Christians belong to denominations that practise infant baptism. The old English word *cristnian,* from which the word 'christening' comes, means 'to make Christian'. This originates from early church practice that teaches that ever since the time of Adam and Eve, everybody has a sinful nature.

> *Surely I was sinful at birth,*
> *sinful from the time my mother conceived me.*
>
> Psalm 51:5 (NIV)

There are no verses in the Bible that indicate christening is wrong as a simple naming ceremony. However, there is no direct evidence to support the practice of christening other than of Jesus directly blessing a baby or child. The idea of a christening ceremony involving the sprinkling (or pouring) of water over an infant to symbolize cleansing from sin is not supported by scripture. It is a mistake to believe that christening can make a baby become a Christian because the Bible teaches that when a child is of an age to understand, they must make their own decision to believe and follow Christ.

The tradition of christening is not biblical, but neither is it forbidden. The danger with the teaching surrounding christening is it can cause confusion because it gives parents, and later in life the child, the mistaken belief that christening makes the child right with God. This can encourage the belief that going through a christening ceremony has in some way made the child adopted into the family of God as a Christian.

Christening should be seen as a journey that parents share with their child so they are able to have an ongoing conversation with them about spiritual issues. Parents should pray with and for their children, as part of learning about the good news of Jesus Christ. Parents should show, by example, how to live a Christian life, and they should encourage the child to learn more about their Christian faith by attending church. The value of having a baby christened is that it shows a commitment to start as you mean to go on.

> *Start children off on the way they should go,*
> *and even when they are old they will not turn from it.*
>
> Proverbs 22:6 (NIV)

The role of parents is to bring their children up to believe in Christ and understand that he is the Son of God and the Saviour of the world.

Christ wants all of us to follow his teaching and lead our lives according to the Bible's commandments.

Fathers, do not exasperate your children; instead, bring them up in the training and instruction of the Lord.

Ephesians 6:4 (NIV)

Dedication

A service of dedication is where the parents bring a baby to be dedicated to God and welcomed into the church fellowship. During a dedication ceremony the parents promise to raise the child in a way consistent with Christ's teaching until the child is old enough to make a decision for themselves to follow Christ and become a Christian. A dedication service may involve the entire family making a public commitment in front of the whole church to set a good example to the child, in line with Christ's teaching.

Children have a special place in the heart of God. Even before a child is born God consecrates them, which means they are very special in his sight.

Before I formed you in the womb I knew you, and before you were born I consecrated you.

Jeremiah 1:5 (NRSV)

The Bible is very clear just how special children are to Jesus. Whilst Jesus was in Judea, crowds of people gathered around him to listen to his teaching ministry and the people were bringing their children to Jesus in order that he would touch them and bless them.[22]

The disciples didn't understand why Jesus loved children so much and tried to discourage them from pestering Jesus. When Jesus realized what his disciples were up to, he told them off.

He said to them, "Let the little children come to me and do not hinder them, for the kingdom of God belongs to such as these. Truly I tell you, anyone who does not receive the kingdom of God like a little child will never enter it." And he took the children in his arms, placed his hands on them and blessed them.

Mark 10:14-6 (NIV)

When Jesus entered the city of Jerusalem and drove out the money-

---

[22] See Mark 10:13

changers and those who were buying and selling, there were a number of disabled people there who were blind and had difficulty walking. After Jesus healed them, the children shouted out, 'Hosanna to the Son of David.'[23] This annoyed the chief priests and scribes and they asked him whether he had heard what the children were chanting? The response from Jesus was robust and unequivocal.

> *"Yes; have you never read (in the Scripture), 'OUT OF THE MOUTHS OF INFANTS AND NURSING BABIES YOU HAVE PREPARED AND PROVIDED PRAISE FOR YOURSELF'?"*
>
> *Matthew 21:16 (AMP)*

Jesus left everyone in no doubt he thought the little children had more understanding and insight than the spiritual leaders of the day. Even the disciples did not really understand the importance of approaching the things of God with the simplicity of a childlike faith.

On another occasion the disciples had the impertinence to ask Jesus who would be the greatest in the kingdom of God. He saw through their pride and envy. Jesus placed a child in front of them and told them that unless they would repent of their sins and become like children, they would never enter the kingdom of heaven; a rebuke which must have come as quite a shock to them!

> *"Therefore, whoever humbles himself like this child is greatest in the kingdom of heaven. Whoever receives and welcomes one child like this in My name receives Me, but whoever causes one of these little ones who believe in Me to stumble and sin (by leading him away from My teaching) it would be better for him to have a heavy millstone (as large as one turned by a donkey) hung around his neck and to be drowned in the depth of the sea."*
>
> *Matthew 18:4-6 (AMP)*

Different modern translations and Bible commentaries help us to appreciate the wider meaning of Scripture. The following explanation helps our understanding of this passage.

> *This is an old question among disciples to this day, who still classify men in the gospel as to position and rewards, contrary*

---

[23] See Matthew 21:15

to the constant rebuke of Christ. In these scriptures He did not rebuke men for expecting a literal earthly kingdom or for wanting to be in it, but He made it clear that entrance into, and place and position in it are on a different basis from that of the world.

Dake's Annotated Reference Bible

There can be no doubt children are a precious gift, so the practice of blessing and dedicating them to the Lord is consistent with biblical practice.

Historically, nothing has changed. Twice in the Old Testament book of Deuteronomy the importance of bringing up babies and young children to respect the law of God is emphasized; the instruction is repeated almost word for word in Deuteronomy 6:7 and 11:19.

> *"These commandments that I give to you today are to be on your hearts. Impress them on your children. Talk about them when you sit at home and when you walk along the road, when you lie down and when you get up."*
>
> Deuteronomy 6:7 (NIV)

At some point each child has to realize they are sinful and need to repent of their sins and make a decision in their own right, when old enough to understand.

> *If you declare with your mouth, "Jesus is Lord," and believe in your heart that God raised him from the dead, you will be saved. For it is with your heart that you believe and are justified, and it is with your mouth that you profess your faith and are saved.*
>
> Romans 10:9-10 (NIV)

The Baptism of Jesus

The Greek word for baptism is *baptizo*, and means 'to immerse, submerge, overwhelm, or make fully wet'. There can be no misunderstanding; baptism means the complete covering of the person and represents the individual dying to self and rising from the grave as a new person. The imagery is meant to represent a new birth.

Christening, Dedication or Baptism?

When John the Baptist preached in the wilderness of Judea, the people came out from Jerusalem, Judea and the Jordan region to be baptized by him.

Confessing their sins, they were baptized by Him in the Jordan River.

Matthew 3:6 (NIV)

It is significant that Jesus appreciated his need to be baptized by John the Baptist, not as a sign of repentance (Jesus alone was completely sinless), but he humbled himself, submitting to the baptism of repentance, because he would take upon himself the sins of the world. When he was crucified, Jesus had no need to be baptized until he became the bearer of all our sins. The late Billy Graham explains that Jesus demonstrated from the beginning of his ministry he was the promised Messiah, 'the Lamb of God who takes away the sin of the world'[24] and that his baptism was a sign of this great truth.

When Jesus initially approached John the Baptist to be baptized, John was very reluctant to baptize him. John recognized he was the Messiah and did not need to be baptized as he was sinless. 'I'm the one who needs to be baptized, not you!'[25] was his response.

John proceeded to baptize Jesus, and following his baptism, a dramatic sign from heaven confirmed this was God's will.

At that moment heaven was opened, the Spirit of God descending like a dove and alighting on him. And a voice from heaven said, "This is my Son, whom I love; with him I am well pleased."

Matthew 3:16-17 (NIV)

After he was baptized, the Holy Spirit entered Jesus and he was led into the wilderness by the Spirit, where he fasted for forty days. The Devil subjected him to several temptations, but he was unyielding.

It is interesting to note that the Bible contains no evidence that during Jesus' ministry he baptized anybody with water. Only his disciples baptized with water, as the Gospel of John confirms.

---

[24] John 1:29 (NIV)
[25] Matthew 3:14 (AMP)

> *Now Jesus learned that the Pharisees heard that he was gaining and baptizing more disciples than John – although in fact it was not Jesus who baptized, but his disciples.*
>
> John 4:1-2 (NIV)

The reason for this was probably two-fold. John said that while he baptized with water for repentance, the Messiah would be coming and 'he will baptize you with the Holy Spirit and fire',[26] which was a different, additional form of baptism: the baptism of the Holy Spirit. The other reason was, Jesus fully understood the fallibility of human nature and wished to avoid jealousy and boasting amongst anyone he baptized, in case some thought baptism by Jesus was in some way superior to baptism by his disciples.

The apostle Paul experienced a similar problem to the one Jesus had anticipated. He expressed relief that he had only baptized a few people, namely Crispus and Gaius and the household of Stephanas. Paul was informed by Chloe's family, who were members of the congregation in the church at Corinth, that there were quarrels and petty jealousies being aired amongst the Christians. Some of the congregation thought it was better to have been baptized by Paul than by Apollos or Cephas, which prompted Paul to say he was glad he did not baptize many in order that 'no one can say you were baptized in my name'[27]. Paul maintained that 'Christ did not send me to baptize, but to preach the gospel'[28]. Paul urged the believers in the church in Corinth to make sure they were united and there were no arguments and divisions amongst them. Their priority was to concentrate on the good news of the gospel and on preaching to those who were spiritually dead and in need of salvation.

What the Bible Says About Baptism

The Bible shows the purpose of baptism is to symbolically emulate the death, burial and resurrection of Jesus Christ. Paul explains in his letter to the Christians in Rome that by repenting of our sins and being baptized, we are dying to our old sinful self and rising from the waters of baptism to a new life in Jesus.

---

[26] Matthew 3:11 (NIV)
[27] 1 Corinthians 1:15 (NIV)
[28] 1 Corinthians 1:17 (NIV)

> *For we know that our old self was crucified with him so that the body ruled by sin might be done away with, that we should no longer be slaves to sin.*
>
> Romans 6:6 (NIV)

Baptism marks the start of a new birth and new beginning for us all. It is relevant to every country irrespective of race and language, because the new commandment is to preach the good news throughout the whole world.

> *For there is no difference between Jew and Gentile – the same Lord is Lord of all and richly blesses all who call on him, for, "Everyone who calls on the name of the Lord will be saved."*
>
> Romans 10:12-13 (NIV)

Paul said the gospel of Jesus Christ now takes precedence over the law of Moses; we are no longer under the law but under grace. It has become the universal gospel.

> *So in Christ Jesus you are all children of God through faith, for all of you who were baptized into Christ have clothed yourselves with Christ. There is neither Jew nor Gentile, neither slave nor free, nor is there male and female, for you are all one in Christ Jesus.*
>
> Galatians 3:28 (NIV)

On the day of Pentecost, when all of the disciples were filled with the Holy Spirit and began speaking in other languages, Peter spoke to the crowds and preached the gospel of repentance, testifying that Jesus Christ was the son of God, the promised Messiah.

> *"Repent and be baptized, every one of you, in the name of Jesus Christ for the forgiveness of your sins. And you will receive the gift of the Holy Spirit. The promise is for you and your children and for all who are far off – for all whom the Lord our God will call."*
>
> Acts 2:38-39 (NIV)

In Chapter 4 we shall look more closely at the what the indwelling or sealing of the Holy Spirit means following conversion and explore what the 'fruit of the Spirit' are, referred to by the apostle Paul in Galatians 5:22. We will also examine what Paul refers to in Acts 11:16 as the experience of being 'baptized with the Holy Spirit' and explain what he describes as the 'spiritual gifts' of the Holy Spirit, of which he clearly states:

> *I do not want you to be uninformed.*
>
> 1 Corinthians 12:1 (AMP)

Meanwhile, we see from the biblical accounts about water baptism that when people repented of their sins and accepted the gift of salvation, this was immediately followed by them being baptized.

This appears not to have presented any practical problems to those being baptized. The average temperatures in Jerusalem in July, its hottest month, is 73°F (23°C), and in the coldest month of January, 46°F (8°C), yet nobody was concerned about catching a chill, such was their enthusiasm to be immediately baptized. When believers are baptized in this country there is usually a delay while the church organizes a baptismal service, complete with a heated baptismal pool!

Repentance and baptism were simultaneous. Once a person had repented of their sins, they were immediately baptized and their sins were figuratively washed away.

Consider this account of Philip who was told by an angel of the Lord to go and meet an important court official, an Ethiopian eunuch, who was returning from Jerusalem on the road to Gaza. He was having difficulty understanding the prophecy of Isaiah which he was reading. Philip caught up with him and explained to him the good news about Jesus, and the eunuch believed and repented. He couldn't wait to get baptized; even before they had completed the journey, the eunuch was asking to be baptized.

> *As they travelled along the road, they came to some water and the eunuch said, "Look, here is water. What can stand in the way of my being baptized?" And he gave orders to stop the chariot. Then both Philip and the eunuch went down into the water and Philip baptized him.*
>
> Acts 8:36-38 (NIV)

We are told that as soon as he had been baptized, Philip was suddenly taken away by the Spirit of the Lord, and the eunuch went on his way rejoicing!

There are many examples in the New Testament of people repenting of their sins and immediately being baptized and receiving the primary anointing gift of the Holy Spirit.

> *Peter said, "Repent (change your old way of thinking, turn from your sinful ways, accept and follow Jesus as the Messiah) and be baptized, each of you, in the name of Jesus Christ because of the forgiveness of your sins; and you will receive the gift of the Holy Spirit. For the promise (of the Holy Spirit) is for you and your children and for all who are far away including the Gentiles), as many as the Lord our God calls to Himself." ... those who accepted his message were baptized; and on that day about three thousand souls were added (to the body of believers)."*
>
> Acts 2:38-39,41 (AMP)

On another occasion, whilst Paul was staying in Macedonia in the city of Philippi, he went outside the city gate to the bank of the River Ganges with the intention of having a time of prayer, but ran into a group of women. One of them, named Lydia, was a dealer in expensive textiles who came from Thyatira. When Paul shared the gospel with her, she responded and 'she and the members of her household were baptized'[29] and she successfully persuaded Paul to stay with her family in her home. Lydia became the first recorded believer in Europe.

Following this encounter with Lydia, Paul and Silas were dragged before the judiciary for healing a slave-girl who had an evil spirit. This spirit enabled her to predict the future and as a fortune-teller she made her owners a great deal of money. When she was healed of the evil spirit, they were furious and dragged Paul and Silas to appear in front of the magistrates. The outcome was, Paul and Silas were severely beaten and thrown into jail and placed in the most secure part of the prison's dungeon, where for good measure their feet were secured in the stocks.

At midnight while Paul and Silas were praising God, there was an earthquake which caused all the prison doors to burst open, and their chains snapped. The commotion that followed woke up the jailer! He knew he had shown dereliction of his duty by failing to comply with the strict instructions from the magistrates to keep Paul and Silas securely. Thinking all the prisoners had escaped, he was about to kill himself with

---

[29] Acts 16:15 (AMP)

Difficult Questions for Christians

his sword, but Paul reassured him that none of the prisoners had escaped. The jailer was shocked but relieved and said, 'Sirs, what must I do to be saved?'[30] Paul was able to tell him the good news: that Jesus Christ, the Messiah, whom they had crucified and buried, had since risen from the dead.

> *"Believe in the Lord Jesus (as your personal Saviour and entrust yourself to Him) and you will be saved, you and your household (if they also believe)."*
>
> Acts 16:31 (AMP)
>
> *Then immediately, he and all his household were baptized. The jailer brought them into his house and set a meal before them; he was filled with joy because he had come to believe in God – he and his whole household.*
>
> Acts 16:33-34 (NIV)

Although we do not know the age or composition of his household, they were old enough to appreciate the need to repent of their sins and were all baptized. The Bible demonstrates there is no age restriction on when a person can be baptized.

Points for Reflection

The Greek word for Bible is *biblia*. It is God's guidebook provided for us and reveals who God is, what his plans are for mankind together with all the prophecies concerning the birth, ministry, death and resurrection of Jesus.

The Bible helps us to live a life pleasing to him and shows us there is only one way to enter the Kingdom of God. It reveals God has a plan for each one of our lives if we come to him and become adopted into his family as full sons and heirs. It is for each person to decide for themselves whether they want to be a believer and follower of Jesus Christ.

Children are very special to God and it is very important that parents bring up their children from an early age to know that God loves them, as well as understanding what the Bible teaches.

Having a church service of dedication or blessing for babies and children is important. It is the wider church family sharing in the responsibility for the child's spiritual development, encouraging the child

---

[30] Acts 16:30 (NIV)

Christening, Dedication or Baptism?

to know the truth about God, so that when old enough to fully understand, they are able to decide to become a follower of Christ. At that point a public declaration of their faith and commitment to follow the Lord by entering the waters of baptism is the next important step on the Christian journey.

Salvation is a necessary precursor to baptism and the Bible teaches public and full immersion by a church leader or disciple of Jesus Christ is the correct path to follow. Incidentally, it is not biblical for a person to baptize themselves and there is no evidence to support such action. Baptism is an important symbol of crucifying the old life, being born again and making a commitment to follow him throughout your life.

> *We were therefore buried with him through baptism into death in order that, just as Christ was raised from the dead through the glory of the Father, we too may live a new life.*
>
> Romans 6:4 (NIV)

We have seen it was quite normal in those days for baptism to immediately follow repentance and often a whole family would be baptized together.

> *Jesus said to them, "Go into all the world and preach the gospel to all creation. Whoever believes and is baptized will be saved, but whoever does not believe will be condemned."*
>
> Mark 16:19 (NIV)

A Personal Challenge

The baptism of children, young people and adults is a public profession of faith and should not be entered into lightly. Many churches encourage those seeking baptism to attend a class to ensure they understand clearly what baptism means. Making a public profession of faith is an important step of faith as you are identifying with Christ's death, burial and resurrection. You are nailing your colours to the mast and declaring you will follow Christ whatever the sacrifice and cost to yourself.

It was not a soft option becoming a Christian. Many suffered persecution and death for their faith and Christians still suffer for their faith. Jesus does not promise an easy ride to his followers and warned his disciples there is a cost in following him.

"If anyone wishes to follow Me (as My disciple), he must deny himself (set aside selfish interests), and take up his cross daily (expressing a willingness to endure whatever may come) and follow me (believing in Me, conforming to My example in living and, if need be, suffering or perhaps dying because of faith in Me)."

Luke 9:23-24 (AMP)

Questions

Should the contemporary church handle requests for christening and baptism differently?

Is it appropriate for a church to impose a minimum age requirement before allowing candidates to be baptized?

How should parents and the church teach a child how to become a Christian?

Is a public profession of faith at the time a person is baptized a suitable safeguard that they understand what baptism really means?

Can improvements be made in this partnership between parents and the church in how it handles the teaching and instruction of children?

Should a child participate in celebrating Communion before they have been baptized?

Chapter Three

Celebrating the Last Supper

Introduction

The celebration of Communion is known by a number of different names: the Last Supper, the Lord's Supper, the Feast of Unleavened Bread, the breaking of bread and the Eucharist.

Although there are differences in how churches understand and celebrate Communion, there is a general appreciation that this is an important celebration and a central part of worship. It is a time to confess your sins to God and remember the crucifixion of the Lord Jesus Christ, his resurrection and the promise of eternal life.

The Eucharist

The expression 'Eucharist' comes from the Greek word *eukharistia*, which means 'thanksgiving' and is another term used to describe the re-enactment of the Last Supper.

Those who celebrate the Holy Eucharist believe the priest, through the power of his ordination and the action of the Holy Spirit, transforms the bread and wine, a process called transubstantiation, a word which derives from the Greek word *metousiosis*. The Roman Catholic church teaches that Jesus Christ is truly present in the Eucharist. They believe that when the sacraments have been consecrated by a priest and the communicants receive the elements of the Eucharist – that is, the sacramental bread and sacramental wine – they actually become the body and blood of Jesus Christ, although they agree they do not taste any different. This teaching is largely based on the following passage in the Gospel of John.

> *"Whoever eats my flesh and drinks my blood has eternal life, and I will raise them up at the last day. For my flesh is real*

food and my blood is real drink. Whoever eats my flesh and drinks my blood remains in me, and I in them."

John 6:54-56 (NIV)

There is a divergence of view about the idea of transubstantiation and many Christians believe that Jesus was speaking symbolically, a view supported by modern translations such as the Amplified Version of the Bible.

The Feast of Passover and Holy Communion

The celebration of Holy Communion symbolizes the coming together of the whole church, known as the 'body of believers', to share in the 'one bread' and to thoughtfully and reverently remember Jesus' sacrifice for the sins of the world.

The celebration of the Last Supper is a public celebration and unites the church as members of the same body. It is important to celebrate Communion in a spirit of humility and gratitude, whilst being aware that taking Communion 'in an unworthy manner' makes an individual liable for punishment by God.[31]

The Feast of Passover, also called *Pesach*, comes from the Hebrew word *pesakh*, meaning 'to pass over'. It celebrates the Israelites gaining their freedom from slavery in Egypt and the creation of their nation under the leadership of Moses.

The Lord had warned Moses that he would bring one more plague on Pharaoh, which would result in the death of every firstborn son and animal in Egypt, including Pharaoh's own son. The Lord gave Moses detailed instructions of how to protect the Israelites from this terrible slaughter by the 'Angel of Death'. They were told to select and sacrifice a spotless lamb and spread its blood on the top and both sides of the doorframes of their houses, so when the Angel of Death saw the blood, he would pass over their houses and their firstborn children would be spared. At midnight the Lord struck down all the firstborn in Egypt and that same night Pharaoh told Moses and Aaron to leave immediately with all the Israelites.

The Bible describes in Exodus 12 how the Israelites had to leave in such a hurry that they were unable to wait for the bread dough to rise (to

---

[31] See page 52, 1 Corinthians 11:27 (NIV)

become leavened bread), which explains why during the seven day Feast of Passover, only 'unleavened bread' is eaten.

The Feast of Unleavened Bread is the first day of the week-long Feast of Passover. During the Feast of Unleavened Bread the Jews eat *matzah* or *matzo* bread, which is a flatbread containing no yeast and is known as the 'bread of affliction'[32]. The *seder* meal is a ritual dinner consumed on the first night of the Feast of Unleavened Bread, and comprises five or six different Passover foods, including *maron,* a bitter herb which symbolizes the bitterness of slavery they experienced in Egypt. Each dish represents a different element of the Exodus story, which is re-enacted during the week of the Passover.

There is a direct link between Passover and Holy Communion because when Jesus shared the Last Supper with his disciples, it was a Passover meal, and Jesus was crucified during Passover. The events of the cross and resurrection are the fulfilment of Passover because Jesus was the spotless Lamb whose blood was shed for the sins of the world. The apostle John recognized this when he met Jesus and said, 'Look, the Lamb of God who takes away the sin of the world.'[33] The apostle Paul also made it clear that the real meaning of Passover is found in Christ when he wrote to the church at Colassae about the festivals and celebrations that took place in the Old Testament.

> *These are a shadow of the things that were to come; the reality, however, is found in Christ.*
>
> Colossians 2:17 (NIV)

He also wrote to the church in Corinth:

> *For Christ, our Passover lamb, has been sacrificed. Therefore let us keep the Festival, not with the old bread leavened with malice and wickedness, but with the unleavened bread of sincerity and truth.*
>
> 1 Corinthians 5:7 (NIV)

Breaking of Bread

'Breaking of bread' is a term used in the New Testament to refer to both the Lord's Supper and the eating of an ordinary meal. The Greek

---

[32] Deuteronomy 16:3 (NIV)
[33] John 1:29 (NIV)

word *klao* means 'to break off pieces' and *artos* means 'bread' or 'loaf'. The phrase 'breaking of bread' clearly refers to the Lord's Supper where 'Jesus took bread, and when he had given thanks, he broke it and gave it to his disciples'[34], and also Jesus 'took bread and broke it and gave it to them'[35].

However, at the feeding of the five thousand, the breaking of bread refers to eating a meal together. Jesus took the five loaves and two fish and 'he gave thanks and broke the loaves'[36].

When Paul was about to be shipwrecked at Malta, they also shared a meal together.

> *He took some bread and gave thanks to God in front of them all, then he broke it and began to eat. They were all encouraged and ate some food themselves. Altogether there were two hundred and seventy-six of us on board.*
>
> Acts 27:35-37 (NIV)

Jesus and the Last Supper

The Last Supper was held on Maundy Thursday, which is the Thursday before Easter. Churches have different views about how the Lord's supper, or Holy Communion, should be celebrated and this explains why practice differs.

At the Last Supper Jesus shared bread and wine with his disciples and instructed them to continue this custom after his death in memory of him. During Communion believers eat a small piece of bread and take a sip of wine (or fruit juice) after they have been blessed or consecrated by the minister.

On the first day of the Passover, known as the Feast of Unleavened Bread, Jesus sent two of his disciples to the city of Jerusalem where he told them they would meet a man carrying a jar of water. They followed him home as Jesus instructed and asked the owner of the house to prepare the guest room for Jesus and the twelve disciples to eat the Passover together.

They were shown to an upper room, exactly as Jesus foretold, and the disciples prepared the Last Supper there. At the agreed time Jesus met

---

[34] Matthew 26:26 (NIV)
[35] Luke 22:19 (NIV)
[36] Mark 6:41 (NIV)

with all his disciples and told them that he was keen to celebrate the Passover with them before he had to suffer, informing them this would be the last time he would be celebrating the Passover with them.

> *And he took bread, and when he had given thanks, he broke it and gave it to them, saying, "This is my body, which is given for you. Do this in remembrance of me." And likewise the cup after they had eaten, saying, "This cup that is poured out for you is the new covenant in my blood."*
>
> Luke 22:19-20 (ESV)

Once they had all shared the unleavened bread and wine, Jesus informed the disciples, 'Truly, I tell you, one of you will betray Me,'[37] and added that the person who was going to betray him was sitting there with them. Jesus said in due course this man would be punished for his act of treachery: 'It would have been better for that man if he had not been born.'[38]

The disciples had no idea that Judas Iscariot would betray Jesus and debated amongst themselves which of them would commit such a treacherous act. The discussion was inconclusive, and Jesus was not prepared to enlighten them. A little later on that discussion gave way to an argument as to who would be the greatest amongst them, until Jesus intervened and reminded them that the greater person is the one who humbles themselves and serves others.

Celebrating the Lovefeast

The practice of celebrating a meal together became known as the Agape Feast or Lovefeast and was a time for believers to have fellowship and share a communal meal, often in their homes. The Eucharist or celebration of Communion was often an integral part of the Lovefeast, as Luke observed.

> *Day by day, as they spent more time together in the temple, they broke bread at home and ate their food with glad and generous hearts, praising God and having the goodwill of all the people.*
>
> Acts 2:46-47 (NRSV)

---

[37] Matthew 26:21 (NIV)
[38] Matthew 26:24 (NIV)

Later on we learn that Paul had to rebuke the church at Corinth for debasing the Lovefeast and celebration of Communion because it had degenerated into an irreverent and shambolic farce.

> *When you come together, it is not really to eat the Lord's supper. For when the time comes to eat, each of you goes ahead with your own supper, and one goes hungry and another becomes drunk. What! Do you not have homes to eat and drink in? Or do you show contempt for the church of God and humiliate those who have nothing? What should I say to you? Should I commend you? In this matter I do not commend you!*
>
> *1 Corinthians 11:20-22 (NRSV)*

It is rare nowadays for a church to have a fellowship meal incorporating Holy Communion as part of an act of worship. The tradition of the Lovefeast incorporating Communion appears to have ceased to be practised sometime after the apostles died, according to early church history, by A.D. 150. Holy Communion is nowadays traditionally incorporated into the normal main service of worship on a Sunday.

Styles of Celebrating Communion

There are considerable differences in how different denominations throughout the world celebrate Communion today. Most churches use wine or alcohol-free wine (wine from which the alcohol has been removed, although trace amounts still remain). It is quite common for grape juice to be used instead of wine, although this was not an option in Jesus' day because grape juice could not be stored without the fermenting process starting.

Some churches celebrate the Eucharist by dipping the bread into the wine, a process known as 'intinction', and the congregation take both sacraments simultaneously. Sharing the cup of wine amongst the congregation is not unhygienic provided the chalice or cup is gold- or silver-plated, as both are antibacterial and wine is antiseptic. However, in those churches that use grape juice, the accepted norm is for individual cups of grape juice to be provided on the grounds it is far more hygienic.

Some Eastern churches use wine but add water to it, which was common practice in the days of the early church, attaching significance to celebrating Communion this way. During the prolonged ordeal of

Difficult Questions for Christians

crucifixion Jesus died, but once it was clear to the soldiers that he was dead, instead of breaking his legs as was the practice to hasten death, 'one of the soldiers pierced his side with a spear, and at once there came out blood and water'[39].

Whilst the use of bread is widespread in celebrating Communion, there are different views on whether leavened or unleavened bread should be used. Unleavened bread is what Jesus used at the Last Supper and some churches use unleavened bread, which often takes the form of a wafer. Churches that use leavened bread often provide a wafer for those who have an allergy to gluten.

Many churches take the view that celebrating Communion is a symbolic act of remembrance that needs to be taken seriously and reverently. The importance of taking Communion can be gauged by the fact Matthew, Mark, Luke, John and Paul all stress the importance of obeying this commandment from Jesus.

> *The Lord Jesus, on the night he was betrayed, took bread, and when he had given thanks, he broke it and said, "This is my body, which is broken for you; do this in remembrance of me." In the same manner he took the cup, saying, "This cup is the new covenant in my blood; do this, whenever you drink it, in remembrance of me."*
>
> 1 Corinthians 11:25 (NIV)

The Bible does not give any specific instruction as to the frequency Communion should be celebrated. It says:

> *For whenever you eat this bread and drink this cup, you proclaim the Lord's death until he comes.*
>
> 1 Corinthians 11:26 (NIV)

The implication is the church should celebrate Communion on a regular basis to renew our focus on Jesus Christ and remember with reverence and a deep sense of gratitude the sacrifice he made for each one of us. Some churches celebrate Communion weekly; others do it as infrequently as every couple of months.

---

[39] John 19:34 (ESV)

Celebrate Communion Anywhere

Communion does not have to be celebrated solely in a church building. Following Pentecost when the early church was established, it was natural for the celebration of Communion to be part of a regular service. Jesus instigated the Last Supper in an upper room in an ordinary house; and in the early church, services of worship took place in the homes of ordinary people.

> *They broke bread in their homes and ate together with glad and sincere hearts praising God and enjoying the favour of the people.*
>
> *Acts 2:46 (NIV)*

Consider the following four examples of house churches.

King Herod was actively persecuting the church in Jerusalem and had recently murdered John's brother James. When the Jews reacted favourably, Herod had Peter arrested and thrown into prison. On the night before his public trial was due to start, the church held a prayer meeting in the home of Mary and were 'gathered together and were praying continually (and had been praying all night)'[40]. Simultaneously, an angel appeared to Peter and miraculously released him from the double chains that bound him to two soldiers. He was led past the sixteen guards allocated to prevent him escaping and out of the prison completely unharmed and through the iron gate leading into the city.

> *He went to the house of Mary the mother of John, also called Mark, where many people had gathered and were praying.*
>
> *Acts 12:12 (NIV)*

On another occasion Paul went to Philippi and met a religious lady named Lydia. All her family responded to Paul's gospel message and became believers and were baptized. Lydia persuaded Paul to stay on with her family at her home. 'If you consider me a believer in the Lord,' she said, 'come and stay at my house,'[41] where in all probability they worshiped and praised the Lord throughout the time Paul stayed with her family.

---

[40] Acts 12:12 (AMP)
[41] See Acts 16:15

On another occasion when Paul was imprisoned for preaching the gospel, he wrote to Philemon asking him to forgive Onesimus, his runaway slave, and accept him back as a Christian brother.

> *To Philemon our dear friend and fellow worker – also to Apphia our sister and Achippus our fellow soldier – and to the church that meets in your home.*
>
> Philemon 1:2 (NIV)

The final example is when Paul signs off his letter to the Corinthians with a greeting from the churches in Asia.

> *Aquila and Priscilla greet you warmly in the Lord, and so does the church that meets at their house.*
>
> 1 Corinthians 16:19 (NIV)

There are no obvious constraints on where Communion can be celebrated.

These precedents are good reasons to celebrate Communion in a believer's home, particularly if they are sick, incapacitated or housebound. Communion can be celebrated in a hospital, a nursing home, a residential home or any other facility, including a penal establishment.

Taking Communion in an Unworthy Manner

Paul gives two warnings about celebrating Communion that need to be taken seriously by all believers in the church.

> *Whoever, therefore, eats the bread or drinks the cup of the Lord in an unworthy manner will be guilty concerning the body and blood of the Lord.*
>
> 1 Corinthians 11:27 (ESV)

The apostle Paul warns that if you do not take this celebration of Communion seriously but treat it flippantly, you become as guilty as those who crucified the Lord Jesus Christ. Some of the Christians in the early church were guilty of treating the Lord's Supper as an excuse to indulge themselves and Paul condemns their behaviour in no uncertain terms, saying that their meetings 'do more harm than good'[42].

---

[42] 1 Corinthians 11:17 (NIV)

Paul criticizes them for allowing divisions to rankle in the church at Corinth. He cites the Lord's supper as an example of how they are making a mockery of this important celebration.

> ...when you meet together, it is not to eat the Lord's Supper, for when you eat, each one hurries to get his own supper first (not waiting for others or the poor). So one goes hungry while another gets drunk.
>
> 1 Corinthians 11:20-21 (AMP)

Paul condemns them for showing 'contempt for the church of God'[43].

> Everyone ought to examine themselves before they eat of the bread and drink from the cup. For those who eat and drink without discerning the body of Christ eat and drink judgment on themselves.
>
> 1 Corinthians 11:28-29 (NIV)

Paul was forthright, explaining that their irreverent and disgraceful behaviour was the reason why many of the congregation were frail and sick and some had even died. By failing to be self-critical and correct their own shortcomings, the church had allowed themselves to be judged and disciplined by the Lord. This should act as a warning to all believers

The New Covenant

Normal practice in the early church was for believers to be baptized immediately and then join the congregation. The practical issues many churches face today mean very few new converts can be baptized quickly, but the church ministry team will encourage a new convert to join the church and to receive instruction and guidance as a new believer, so they can grow spiritually.

Baptism is a public confession of faith and meets all the scriptural criteria to participate in the Lord's Supper. Some churches take the view that even though a person is a believer, they must be baptized before celebrating Communion.

Paul told the church, everyone who shares the Lord's Supper must be believers who recognize they are sinners and have repented of their sins. They must appreciate their need for a Saviour and have asked God for

---

[43] 1 Corinthians 11:22 (NRSV)

forgiveness by putting their trust in Jesus Christ. If a child, young person or adult meets that criteria, then it becomes a matter for the individual, or in the case of a child for the parents, to decide if it is appropriate for them to share in the Lord's Supper.

The Amplified Version of the Bible is helpful in clarifying this important scripture.

> *But a person must (prayerfully) examine himself (and his relationship to Christ) and only when he has done so should he eat of the bread and drink of the cup. For anyone who drinks (without solemn reverence and heartfelt gratitude for the sacrifice of Christ) eats and drinks a judgment on himself.*
> *1 Corinthians 11:28-29 (AMP)*

Communion is the new covenant given by God to all believers. The old covenant was given by God to the Israelites when they were freed from slavery in Egypt, and required them to make regular sacrifices to God to atone for their sins.

> *'Truly, truly, I say to you, whoever believes has eternal life. I am the bread of life. Your fathers ate the manna in the wilderness, and they died. This is the bread that comes down from heaven, so that one may eat of it and not die. I am the living bread that came down from heaven. If anyone eats of this bread, he will live forever. And the bread I give for the life of the world is my flesh.'*
> *John 6:47-51 (ESV)*

Points for Reflection

To avoid being guilty of taking Communion in an unworthy manner, the following advice should be followed before participating in the Lord's Supper.

1. Celebrating the Lord's Supper is for all believers who love the Lord. There is no restriction in the Bible on eligibility, but it is important that everyone who receives Communion understands its significance. If you are a non-believer and take Communion

without repenting of your sins, you are taking the bread and wine in an 'unworthy manner'[44].

2. Pray and confess any sin to the Lord before taking Communion and meditate on the ultimate sacrifice Christ made for your sins. A believer should not refuse to celebrate Communion because they genuinely feel unworthy, for we all are sinners and unworthy, but instead be thankful they are a sinner saved by grace.

> *By grace you are saved through faith – and this not from yourselves, it is the gift of God – not by works, so that no one can boast.*
>
> *Ephesians 2:8 (NIV)*

3. Consider whether you have a dispute or an unresolved problem with another Christian brother. 'First go and be reconciled to them.'[45] Our attitude towards other believers should not be judgmental but forgiving and Christ-like.

4. Unless there is a medical reason, you should take both of the sacraments, because the bread represents his body broken for you and the wine or grape juice represents his blood shed for your sins.[46]

A Personal Challenge

The church is made up of flawed people including each one of us. Jesus loves the church despite all its faults, because it is his bride. We should also love his church and love all of its members, because Jesus loved us enough to die for our sins. We can develop a growing love for other believers in the church by exercising patience, through prayer and perseverance.

> *Husbands love your wives, just as Christ also loved the church and gave himself up for her, to make her holy, cleansing her by the washing with water through the word and to present*

---

[44] 1 Corinthians 11:27 (ESV)
[45] Matthew 5:24 (NIV)
[46] See 1 Corinthians 11:26

her to himself as a radiant church, without stain or wrinkle or any other blemish, but holy and blameless.
Ephesians 5:25-27 (NIV)

Celebrating the Last Supper

Questions

Should a person living with a same-sex partner celebrate Communion?

How should a believer act if they know a communicant is guilty of a serious breach of God's commandments?

Can transubstantiation be reconciled with the words of Jesus concerning taking Communion?

Does the practice of celebrating Communion in your church contradict the Bible's teaching, and if so, how should you respond?

How can we ensure we are not taking Communion in a 'unworthy manner'?

Should a believer who was christened as a baby be baptized before they celebrate Communion?

Chapter Four

Are Christians Really Any Different?

It is fair to say there is considerable confusion in the church today over what it means to be anointed or sealed by the Holy Spirit and how a person becomes filled with the Holy Spirit. Some argue that these distinctions are unimportant because Christians do not appear to be any different to anybody else. We shall examine how once a person becomes a Christian, some very significant changes occur after the Holy Spirit enters that person's life, and how this should be apparent to everyone in the way they behave and live their life.

In the Old Testament the kings and priests were physically anointed with oil to show they were set apart.

> *"Anoint Aaron and his sons and consecrate them, so they may serve me as priests. Say to the Israelites, 'This is to be my sacred anointing oil for the generations to come.'"*
>
> Exodus 30:30-31 (NIV)

The temple was also anointed to show it was holy.

> *"Take the anointing oil and anoint the tabernacle and everything in it."*
>
> Exodus 40:9 (NIV)

In the new covenant all Christians are anointed and are sealed by the Holy Spirit when they repent of their sin and became believers. You are chosen and set apart in the same way the kings and priests were special and set apart. Every Christian is now the equivalent spiritually of an Old Testament priest.

> *You are a chosen people, a royal priesthood, a holy nation, God's special possession.*
>
> 1 Peter 2:9 (NIV)

> ...the anointing that you received from Him abides in you...
>
> 1 John 2:27 (NRSV)

There is a condition if you wish to keep the anointing you received when you become a Christian.

> "I am the vine; you are the branches. If you remain in me and I in you, you will bear much fruit; apart from me you can do nothing. If you do not remain in me, you are like a branch that is thrown away and withers; such branches are picked up, thrown into the fire and burned."
>
> John 15:4-6 (NIV)

The Holy Trinity

Unlike the religion of Islam that is a monotheistic faith (the belief in only one God), most Christian denominations believe in the Holy Trinity. A triune God is traditionally explained as 'one God in three persons'. The doctrine of the Trinity is the belief that God is one God, but three coeternal consubstantial persons (of one and the same substance) – the Father, the Son (Jesus Christ) and the Holy Spirit – as one God in three Divine Persons.

Paul explains to the church at Corinth the different roles of 'God, the Father' and the 'Lord, Jesus Christ':

> *Yet for us there is one God, the Father, from whom are all things and for whom we exist, and one Lord, Jesus Christ, through whom are all things and through whom we exist. However, not all possess this knowledge.*
>
> 1 Corinthians 8:6-7 (ESV)

When Jesus was baptized by John the Baptist, as soon as he came up out of the water heaven opened and the Spirit of God descended like a dove and rested on Jesus and 'and a voice from heaven said, "This is my Son, whom I love; with him I am well pleased."'[47]

The Greek word *parakletos* means 'advocate' or 'intercessor'. Jesus promised to send his disciples the Holy Spirit after he had ascended back to his Father.

---

[47] Matthew 3:17 (NIV)

> "All this I have spoken while still with you. But the Advocate, the Holy Spirit, whom the Father will send in my name, will teach you all things and will remind you of everything I have said to you."
>
> *John 14:25-26 (NIV)*

After the resurrection, Jesus met the eleven disciples at a mountain near Galilee and gave them what is known as the Great Commission.

> "Go therefore and make disciples of all nations, baptizing them in the name of the Father and of the Son and of the Holy Spirit, teaching them to observe all that I have commanded you."
>
> *Matthew 28:18-20 (NIV)*

In his book *Angels – God's Secret Agents*, Billy Graham says:

> ...the doctrine of the Trinity was one of the most complex problems I had to encounter and I never fully resolved it, for it contains an aspect of mystery. I accept it as a revelation of God.

The Primary Anointing or Sealing of the Holy Spirit

There are a number of expressions used to describe the primary anointing or the indwelling presence of the Holy Spirit. Paul describes it as being 'sealed' with the Holy Spirit or being filled with the Holy Spirit.

> In Him you also, when you heard the word of truth, the gospel of your salvation, and believed in Him, were sealed with the promised Holy Spirit, who is the guarantee of our inheritance until we acquire possession of it, to the praise of his glory.
>
> *Ephesians 1:13 (ESV)*

This means that the sealing of the Holy Spirit takes place at the point of salvation and is a promise and guarantee that we will spend eternity with Jesus Christ.

> The Spirit you received does not make you slaves, so that you live in fear again; rather, the Spirit you received brought about your adoption to sonship. And by him we cry, "Abba, Father."[2]
>
> *Romans 8:15 (NIV)*

The Greek word *shragizo* means 'to set a seal upon, mark with a seal'. Hot wax would be used as a seal to guarantee a document or letter. Everyone in the Roman Empire would have had their own personal seal (rather like a signature today) that guaranteed security and indicated ownership.[48]

Sealing a document protected the integrity of the contents until the correct recipient broke the seal.

> *The king removed his signet ring from his hand (that is, the special ring which was used to seal his letters) and gave it to Haman, the son of Hammedatha the Agagite, the enemy of the Jews.*
>
> Esther 3:10 (AMP)

The seal was also used to protect against tampering, as in the case when Pilate instructed the soldiers to guard and seal the tomb of Jesus.

> *So they went and made the tomb secure, and along with (stationing) a guard of soldiers (to be on watch) they set a seal on the stone.*
>
> Matthew 27:66 (AMP)

When we become believers and are born again, we reject our sinful nature.

> *Do not get drunk on wine, which leads to wickedness (corruption, stupidity), but be filled with the (Holy) Spirit and constantly guided by Him.*
>
> Ephesians 5:18 (AMP)

The Bible points out our 'old nature' or 'ego' is diametrically opposed to the Holy Spirit, and Paul reminds us of our natural rebellious tendencies.

> *Now the practices of the sinful nature are clearly evident: they are sexual immorality, impurity, sensuality (total irresponsibility, lack of self-control), idolatry, sorcery, hostility, strife, jealously, fits of anger, disputes, dissensions, factions (that*

---

[48] cp. Song of Solomon 8:6

> *promote heresies), envy, drunkenness, riotous behaviour, and other things like these.*
>
> Galatians 5:19-21 (AMP)

The Bible is very clear: if you live like this you will not go to heaven and be with God for eternity but suffer judgment and punishment. One of the functions of the Holy Spirit is to convince the individual they are a sinner. The Holy Spirit troubles your conscience until you finally recognize you are a sinner and become ashamed of your sin.

> *"When he comes, he will prove the world to be in the wrong about sin and righteousness and judgment: about sin, because people do not believe in me."*
>
> John 16:8 (NIV)

The Greek word for 'repent' is *metanoeo* which means 'to change one's mind' and turn around from not seeking to do God's will, to decide to do God's will. Repenting of one's sins is the first stage to becoming a believer. If you are truly sorry and ask God for forgiveness, the Holy Spirit will help you to become a believer. Once you receive God's forgiveness and accept Jesus Christ as your personal Saviour, you become 'born again' to a new life in Jesus and adopted into his family as a child of God.

> *"Repent and be baptized, every one of you, in the name of Jesus Christ for the forgiveness of your sins. And you will receive the gift of the Holy Spirit."*
>
> Acts 2:38 (NIV)

The apostle Paul tells us it is important to value this gift we have received and not to cause the Holy Spirit any reason to feel sadness and disappointment as a result of the way we have behaved.

> *And do not grieve the Holy Spirit of God (but seek to please Him), by whom you were sealed and marked (branded as God's own) for the day of redemption.*
>
> Ephesians 4:30 (NIV)

We grieve the Holy Spirit when we fail to get rid of bitterness, anger, resentment, or continually find fault in others, are antagonistic, act spitefully and verbally abuse others. Instead we are to be kind, helpful and compassionate to each other, forgiving one another and always remembering how the Lord forgave us. Once a person surrenders their life to Christ and becomes a believer and follower of Jesus Christ, they receive the gift of the Holy Spirit, which is the primary anointing or seal of the Holy Spirit.

The Fruit of the Spirit

Once you commit your life to Christ and become born again, the Spirit of God will immediately help you to produce the 'fruit of the Spirit.' Initially when you surrender your life to Christ, you receive the seeds of the fruit of the Spirit. The seed has been planted into good soil and if nourished and fertilised will in time produce a harvest of good fruit. Jesus said that 'the seed is the word of God'[49].

> *"But the seed on good soil stands for those with a noble and good heart, who hear the word, retain it, and by persevering produce a crop."*
>
> *Luke 8:15 (NIV)*

When you decide to surrender your life fully to the Holy Spirit, this allows God through the work of his Holy Spirit to help you become the person he wants you to be.

> *I cannot bear the fruit of the Spirit by my own strength. I cannot love. I have no power. But this Holy Spirit, who lives in me since I received Christ as my Saviour, is the one who gives me the power to love. He gives me the joy. He gives me the peace. He gives me the patience. He bears the fruit in my life.*
>
> *Billy Graham*

The Apostle Paul emphasized that the new covenant is based entirely on the commandment, 'You shall love your neighbour as yourself,'[50] and identified nine attributes of a true Christian which are known as 'the fruit of the Spirit'.

> *But the fruit of the Spirit is love, joy, peace, patience, kindness, goodness, faithfulness, gentleness, self-control.*
>
> *Galatians 5:22 (ESV)*

---

[49] Luke 8:11 (NIV)
[50] See Galatians 5:14

Live in Harmony With God

The first three 'fruit of the Spirit' are love, joy and peace. These important 'fruit of the Spirit' are what the believer needs to live in perfect harmony with God.

LOVE

There are four words to describe love in the Greek whereas in the English language there is only one. In Greek, *eros* is sensual or romantic love. *Storge* is the word used to describe the love that develops naturally in families between parents and children and between brothers and sisters, such as the *storge* love sisters Mary and Martha had for their brother Lazarus. *Philia* love describes the love between a husband and wife or is used to convey the concept of brotherly love that unites believers, unique to Christianity. *Philia* love was what Jesus described as being a recognizable characteristic of his followers.

> *"By this everyone will know that you are my disciples, if you love one another."*
>
> John 13:35 (NIV)

Agape love is the highest form of love because it describes God's supernatural love for us; perfect, unconditional, immeasurable, sacrificial love, which Jesus demonstrated in his life, death and resurrection.

> *Love is patient, love is kind. It does not envy, it does not boast. It does not dishonor others, it is not self-seeking, it is not easily angered, it keeps no record of wrongs. Love does not delight in evil but rejoices with the truth. It always protects, always trusts, always hopes, always perseveres. Love never fails.*
>
> 1 Corinthians 13:4-8 (NIV)

JOY

The Greek word is *chara,* which is an inner gladness or delight.

> *...the joy of the LORD is your strength.*
>
> Nehemiah 8:10 (NIV)

The writer of Hebrews urges us not to get distracted but to focus our attention on Jesus who joyfully went to the cross to pay the price for our sins.

> *Let us run with perseverance the race marked out for us, fixing our eyes on Jesus, the pioneer and perfecter of faith. For the joy set before him, he endured the cross, scorning its shame, and sat down at the right hand of the throne of God.*
>
> Hebrews 12:1-2 (NIV)

PEACE

The Greek word is *eireinei,* which refers to a tranquil state of a mind at perfect rest.

> *And the peace of God (that peace which reassures the heart, that peace) which transcends all understanding, (that peace which) stands guard over your hearts and your minds in Christ Jesus (is yours).*
>
> Philippians 4:7 (AMP)

Life in Harmony With Others

The next three 'fruit of the Spirit' are patience, kindness and goodness. These are the fruits we need to live in harmony with other people.

PATIENCE

The Greek word is *makrothumia*, which means 'endurance and steadfastness'.

> *Patience is not simply the ability to wait but how we behave while we're waiting.*
>
> Joyce Meyer

The story of Abraham and Sarah is a great example of how God keeps his promises, even when it appears humanly impossible. We should never doubt God's promises because God will do things according to his divine plan.

> *When God made his promise to Abraham, he swore by himself, saying, "I will surely bless you and give you many descendants."*
>
> Hebrews 6:14 (NIV)

It didn't come immediately, as we shall see. Abraham had to wait well over a decade before God fulfilled his promise to give him a son, by which time it was clearly a miracle. When Abraham was in his eighties he had a vision from God who again promised he would have a son and many descendants.

> *"Look at the sky. Count the stars. Can you do it? Count your descendants! You're going to have a big family, Abram!" And he believed! Believed God.*
>
> *Genesis 15:5 (MSG)*

However, Sarah became impatient, perhaps understandably, as over a decade had elapsed since Abraham had received the vision, and she felt God had not kept his word. She came up with a plan and persuaded Abraham to marry Hagar, her Egyptian maid, who became pregnant. Hagar gave birth to a son whom they named Ishmael – by which time Abraham was eighty-six years old. Impatience led Abraham and Sarah to take things into their own hands, but this had serious repercussions and seriously fractured the relationship between Sarah and Hagar. It became so serious that that an angel had to intervene!

When Abraham was ninety-nine years old and Sarah his wife was ninety, God again promised Abraham, 'You will be the father of many nations,'[51] and, 'I will bless her and surely give you a son by her. I will bless her so that she will be the mother of many nations.'[52]

Later on, the Lord appeared to Abraham by sending three angels to him. One of them said, 'I will surely return to you about this time next year, and Sarah your wife will have a son.'[53] As promised, Sarah became pregnant and 'Abraham was a hundred years old when his son Isaac was born'[54].

Patience is essential if you are to combat frustration. Developing patience is the way to maintain a healthy mind, because anger and stress can wreck your health and peace of mind and are a major cause of mental health problems facing people today.

---

[51] Genesis 17:4 (NIV)
[52] Genesis 17:16 (NIV)
[53] Genesis 18:10 (NIV)
[54] Genesis 21:5 (NIV)

> *Quiet down before God, be prayerful before him. Don't bother with those who climb the ladder, who elbow their way to the top.*
>
> Psalm 37:7 (MSG)

Life can be a rat-race, as the psalmist appreciated thousands of years ago. Human nature has not changed over the centuries; Satan sees to that. Christ did not promise us an easy ride when we become believers and follow him. He said we would experience trouble, sickness and distress, but if we pray, seeking comfort and guidance, he will give us the strength to persevere. Paul urges us to be 'constantly rejoicing in hope (because of our confidence in Christ), steadfast and patient in distress, devoted to prayer (continually seeking wisdom, guidance, and strength)'[55].

KINDNESS

This is a word with several meanings in the English: friendly, generous and considerate. Similarly in Greek, the word *chrestotes* means being good, kind, friendly, respecting and helping others.

> *Be kind and helpful to one another, tender-hearted (compassionate, understanding), forgiving one another (readily and freely), just as God in Christ also forgave you.*
>
> Ephesians 4:32 (AMP)

Eleemon means 'to be merciful to others'. God's kindness is intended to lead to repentance and can release the believer from disease, fear or trouble. God says that we should be kind and show mercy to other people because kindness is more important than performing sacrifices.

> *"Go and learn what this means: 'I desire mercy, not sacrifice.' For I have not come to call the righteous, but sinners."*
>
> Matthew 9:13 (NIV)

GOODNESS

The Greek word is *agathosune* and describes the character of a person who is honest, upright and has integrity. In the Sermon on the Mount, Jesus said:

---

[55] Romans 12:12 (AMP)

"In the same way, let your light shine before others, that they may see your good deeds and glorify your Father in heaven."
Matthew 5:16 (NIV)

Live at Peace With Yourself

The final three 'fruit of the spirit' are faithfulness, gentleness and self-control. These fruit are necessary in order to have a good relationship where you are at peace with yourself.

FAITHFULNESS

The Greek word is *pistis* and means 'trustworthy, reliable and dependable'. Biblical faithfulness means believing what the Bible says about God's universe, his existence, his actions and his character. We are called to be faithful, as the writer of Hebrews reminds us in the following examples.

- Abel offered a more acceptable sacrifice than Cain (11:4).
- Enoch did not see death because he pleased God (11:5).
- Noah trusted God about the forthcoming judgment and constructed his ark in order to save his family (11:7).
- Abraham went where God called him to receive his inheritance (11:8).
- Sarah, his wife, conceived a promised son (11:11).
- Abraham offered his only son Isaac as a sacrifice believing God would raise him from the dead (11:17).
- Isaac blessed Jacob and Esau believing God's revelation to him about events to come (11:20).
- Jacob, when he was dying, blessed each of Joseph's sons (11:21).
- When Joseph was dying, he reminded his sons of God's promise to deliver the Israelites from slavery in Egypt and in faith he instructed them to bury him in the promised land (11:22).
- Moses was hidden for three months by his parents in defiance of Pharaoh's order that all male Hebrew babies were to be thrown into the River Nile (11:23).

- Moses refused to be treated as the son of Pharaoh's daughter but chose to share the hardship with his people (11:26).

- Moses left Egypt, unafraid of the furious King Pharaoh (11:27).

- Moses celebrated the Passover and the sprinkling of blood on the doorposts to protect the firstborn of each Jewish household (11:28).

- The Israelites crossed the Red Sea unharmed and on dry land, by faith, but when the Egyptians attempted to cross, they were all drowned (11:29).

- The walls of Jericho fell down when Joshua and the Israelites marched around them for seven days (11:30).

- Rahab the prostitute, who welcomed the spies, was saved from death (11:31).

The Hebrews writer says there were many more examples, like Barak, who responded to the prophetess Deborah and summoned his army to defeat Sisera, destroying every one of his nine hundred chariots in the ensuing battle.[56] Jephthah challenged the Ammonites and defeated them, then became their leader for six years, but rashly made a vow to God which resulted in the death of his daughter.[57] Others included Gideon, David and Samuel and the prophets.[58]

The apostle Paul writes to the church in Corinth with words of encouragement.

For we walk by faith, not sight (living in our lives in a manner consistent with our belief in God's promises.)

2 Corinthians 5:7 (AMP)

The Hebrew writer reminds the believers in the church at Rome that it is impossible to please God without exercising faith.

---

[56] See Judges 4:4-16
[57] See Judges 11:4-33
[58] See Hebrews 11:32-34

Difficult Questions for Christians

> *Without faith it is impossible to please Him, for whoever would draw near to God must believe that he exists and that he rewards those who seek him.*
>
> *Hebrews 11:6 (ESV)*

There is a warning in Mark's Gospel that faith is crucial to the work of the Holy Spirit. Even Jesus was unable to work miracles in his hometown of Nazareth due to their disbelief and lack of faith.

> *He could not do miracles there at all (because of their unbelief) except that He laid hands on a few sick people and healed them. He wondered at their unbelief.*
>
> *Mark 6:6 (AMP)*

GENTLENESS

The Greek word is *prautes,* which describes an even-tempered individual who has their emotions under control. We are 'to speak evil of no one, to avoid quarrelling, to be gentle, and to show perfect courtesy towards all people'[59].

It is imperative that as Christians we act with restraint, avoid heated arguments and act Christ-like even when people speak maliciously about us and spread lies. If our attitude is gentle and respectful, our critics may later feel ashamed of their behaviour and the Holy Spirit may convince them of the need to repent.

> *Always be prepared to give an answer to everyone who asks you to give a reason for the hope that you have. But do this with gentleness and respect.*
>
> *1 Peter 3:15 (NIV)*

SELF-CONTROL

The Greek word is *egkrateia,* which means 'the ability to exercise self-restraint'. The believer is warned that failing to exercise self-control makes us slaves to whatever controls us; be it power, money, lust or self-gratification. Self-control is essential to living a holy life that brings glory to God. When Paul wrote to Timothy, he urged him to fan into flame the gift of God.

---

[59] Titus 3:2 (ESV)

> *...the Spirit God gave us does not make us timid, but gives us power, love and self-discipline.*
>
> 2 Timothy 1:7 (NIV)

Self-control can be developed by immersing ourselves in the Bible and allowing the Holy Spirit to guide us whenever we face temptation.

> *Little children, you are from God and have overcome them. He who is in you is greater than he [Satan] who is in the world.*
>
> 1 John 4:4 (ESV)

The truth is, we have already won because Satan is a defeated enemy. The Holy Spirit will always win our battles if we place our trust in him and allow his power to fill our lives.

Points for Reflection

A person who becomes a believer will receive the indwelling of the Holy Spirit and the apostle Paul points out that as we walk in the Spirit, the 'fruit of the Spirit' will grow.

> *So I say, walk by the Spirit, and you will not gratify the desires of the flesh. For the flesh desires what is contrary to the Spirit, and the Spirit what is contrary to the flesh. They are in conflict with each other, so you are not to do whatever you want.*
>
> Galatians 5:16-17 (NIV)

Once we become a Christian we are no longer under the law of Moses, because when we examine the Ten Commandments, we realize we can never fully comply with God's standards. Since we became followers of Jesus Christ we are under grace, and by letting the indwelling Holy Spirit be our guide, he helps us choose to do what is right and pleasing to him. When believers surrender their lives to the Holy Spirit, their lives increasingly become fruitful and they become a blessing to others in the church family.

The gifts of the Holy Spirit cannot operate effectively in the church without the 'fruit of the Spirit' being apparent in the life of the believer. As we examine the range of spiritual gifts that God gives to Christians, it becomes apparent that their purpose is to make believers in the church stronger and to give them the power to witness effectively.

Difficult Questions for Christians

Questions

How can I become more fruitful as a Christian?

Why do some of my non-Christian friends appear to have more 'fruit' in their lives than believers do?

How can I help other believers in our church to be more fruitful?

Which 'fruit of the Spirit' is the most important to develop?

How do I obtain spiritual gifts?

Some of my Christian friends are an embarrassment to me because of the way they behave when they are not in church. What can I do?

Chapter Five

Are Spiritual Gifts Relevant Today?

The nine 'fruit of the Spirit'[60] should be apparent in every Christian who has accepted Christ as their Saviour. The gifts of the Spirit are different. Everyone who becomes a Christian has the indwelling or seal of the Holy Spirit. The outpouring or baptism of the Holy Spirit is the power that enables us to witness and lead others to belief in Jesus Christ.

In what is known as the Great Commission, Jesus told his disciples:

> *"All authority in heaven and on earth has been given to me. Therefore go and make disciples of all nations, baptizing them in the name of the Father and of the Son and of the Holy Spirit and teaching them to obey everything I have commanded you."*
>
> Matthew 28:19 (NIV)

Not every Christian who is baptized in the Holy Spirit has the same gifts as another Christian because God distributes his gifts as he thinks appropriate.

Spiritual Gifts of the Holy Spirit

The 'gifts of the Spirit' are provided to build up the church, referred to as the body.

> *...the body is not made up of one part but of many.*
>
> 1 Corinthians 12:14 (NIV)

Every part of the body is essential to the well-being of the whole person, even those parts that appear to be less important. 'If one part

---

[60] See Galatians 5:22-23

suffers, every part suffers with it,'[61] as you know only too well if you have toothache or bang your thumb with a hammer.

The Apostle Paul says God values some spiritual gifts more highly in the church.

> *First of all apostles, second prophets and third teachers, then miracles, then gifts of healing, of helping, of guidance, and of different tongues.*
>
> 1 Corinthians 12:28 (NIV)

The emphasis is on a variety of 'gifts of the Spirit', so the church is blessed and enriched when a variety of spiritual gifts are in operation.

The Nine Supernatural Gifts of the Holy Spirit

Paul says there are different kinds of gifts, but they are all given to strengthen the church and bring people to a saving knowledge of the Lord Jesus Christ.

> *To one is given through the Spirit the utterance of wisdom, and to another the utterance of knowledge according to the same Spirit, to another faith by the same Spirit, to another gifts of healing by the one Spirit, to another the working of miracles, to another prophecy, to another the discernment of spirits, to another various kinds of tongues, to another the interpretation of tongues. All these are activated by one and the same Spirit, who allots to each one individually just as the Spirit chooses.*
>
> 1 Corinthians 12:8-11 (NRSV)

However, Paul makes the point forcibly in 1 Corinthians 13 that the gifts are of little value to the church or anybody else if they are exercised without love. He urges us to ensure our motives are unselfish and not self-seeking; that we are not trying to show off or make out that we are spiritually superior to others who have not been blessed by God with a particular spiritual gift.

> *If I speak with the tongues of men and or angels, but have not love (for others growing out of God's love for me), then I have become only a noisy gong or a clanging cymbal (just an*

---

[61] 1 Corinthians 12:26 (NIV)

annoying distraction). And if I have the gift of prophecy (and speak a new message from God to the people), and understand all mysteries and (possess) all knowledge; and if I have all (sufficient) faith so that I can remove mountains, but do not have love (reaching out to others), I am nothing. If I give all my possessions to feed the poor and if I surrender my body to be burned, but do not have love, it does me no good at all.

1 Corinthians 13:1-3 (AMP)

THE WORD OF WISDOM

In the Greek the word *sophia* means 'wisdom'. The gift of wisdom is the ability to understand and speak out biblical truth so that it can be applied to given situations.

THE WORD OF KNOWLEDGE

In the Greek the word *gnosis* means 'seeking to know'. This is a speaking gift that involves understanding truth and circumstances, using insight that comes from God who reveals it to the speaker.

FAITH

In the Greek the word *pistis* means 'of firm persuasion or conviction'. This gift is the ability to know God's power and promises to achieve his will and purpose. The believer with this gift has an unshakeable belief in God and biblical truths, so whatever circumstances and challenges they face, their confidence in God is not shaken.

GIFTS OF HEALING

In the Greek the word *iama* means 'a cure' or 'to make whole'. These gifts were used by God to make people whole from physical, emotional, mental or spiritual conditions. The gifts of healing (note the plural) means there are different kinds of healing ministries. These gifts were regularly exercised by the apostles in the early church, including raising people from the dead. Peter raised Tabitha from the dead in the town of Lydda; in Greek her name was Dorcas.

Turning towards the dead woman, he said, "Tabitha get up." She opened her eyes and seeing Peter she sat up.

Acts 9:40 (NIV)

Difficult Questions for Christians

A man called Eutychus was raised from the dead in Troas by Paul. This unfortunate man fell asleep during one of his long sermons which lasted until midnight.

> ...he fell to the ground from the third story and was picked up dead.
>
> Acts 20:9 (NIV)

Interestingly, Luke records that after Eutychus was raised from the dead Paul returned and 'after talking until daylight, he left'[62].

MIRACLES

These are an act of divine intervention by God in the natural laws of the universe. In the Bible Jesus turned water into wine[63] and fed five thousand Jewish people with five loaves and two fish[64] and later fed four thousand Gentiles with seven loaves and a few fish.[65] God parted the Red Sea,[66] Daniel emerged unscathed when thrown into the lion's den[67] and Peter left the fishing boat and walked on water to Jesus, until his faith failed him.[68] Miracles are unexplained events that occur which witnesses recognize and acknowledge to be of supernatural origin.

PROPHECY

In the Greek the word *prophetes* means 'the forthtelling of the will of God'. This is when a direct and clear prophetic word from the Lord is received to give to someone.

The one who prophesies speaks to people for their strengthening encouraging and comfort. The one who prophesies edifies (meaning uplifts or builds) the church.[69]

Prophecies can cover a wide range of issues, which can include predicting future events or giving someone encouragement which helps

---

[62] Acts 20:11 (NIV)
[63] See John 2
[64] See Mark 6
[65] See Mark 8
[66] See Exodus 14
[67] See Daniel 6
[68] See Matthew 14
[69] See 1 Corinthians 14:4

Are Spiritual Gifts Relevant Today?

them with a specific issue they are facing. Paul advises us to treat prophecy with respect but to test it for authenticity.

> *Do not treat prophecies with contempt but test them all; hold on to what is good, reject every kind of evil.*
>
> *1 Thessalonians 5:19-21 (NIV)*

The Bible warns us to watch out for false prophets, who are like a wolf in sheep's clothing, and urges us to apply the test of true spirituality.

> *By their fruit you will recognize them.*
>
> *Matthew 7:16 (NIV)*

DISCERNING OF SPIRITS

In the Greek the word *diakrisis* means 'to separate thoroughly or discriminate'. This gift of the Holy Spirit is supernatural discernment, which is an ability to distinguish truth from error and have insight and knowledge regarding three types of spirit. These are demonic spirits, God's angels and human spirits. In the book *Brain, Consciousness and God*, Daniel A. Helminiak states:

> *...the human spirit is considered to be the mental functions of awareness, insight, understanding, judgement and other reasoning powers.*

In the case of demonic spirits, Jesus and the apostles regularly discerned the presence of demonic spirits and cast them out of tormented souls. It should be stressed that the gift of discernment needs to be operating before any exorcism and healing can take place.

Another spirit force at work are God's angels, who are ministering spirits. Throughout history angels have appeared to people on special occasions. The Bible warns us that Satan and his demons can impersonate them and appear as an 'angel of light'[70]. False religions like Islam and Mormonism were started by false angels who appeared and deceived Muhammad and Joseph Smith. The Bible teaches how false spirits can be identified.

> *Many false prophets have gone out into the world. This is how you can recognize the Spirit of God: Every spirit that acknowledges that Jesus Christ has come in the flesh is from*

---

[70] 2 Corinthians 11:4 (NIV)

> *God, but every spirit that does not acknowledge Jesus is not from God. This is the spirit of the antichrist, which you have heard is coming and even now is already in the world.*
>
> 1 John 4:2-3 (NIV)

The apostle Paul writing to the church at Corinth warns them about 'false apostles, deceitful workers masquerading as apostles of Christ'[71] and explains that the spiritual gift of 'discernment of spirits'[72] is the ability to distinguish sound, godly doctrine from the deceptive doctrine of man-made religions and cults. Believers are told to be cautious and careful, and not to believe every spirit, but to 'test the spirits to see whether they are from God'[73]. Exercising the ability to distinguish between spirits will enable the church and believers to 'recognise the Spirit of truth and the Spirit of falsehood'[74].

DIFFERENT KINDS OF TONGUES

In the Greek the word *glossa* means 'the tongue'. This is the supernatural ability to speak in a heavenly language or in foreign languages previously unknown to the speaker, in order to pray effectively.

It may be that you do not know what or how to pray in a given situation; then, exercising the gift of 'speaking in different kinds of tongues'[75] bypasses the natural voice and the Holy Spirit intercedes directly with God the Father – and nobody else outside the Godhead hears your prayer. Praying in tongues in private is a way of praising, worshipping and 'giving thanks well enough (in a way that God is glorified)'[76].

> *In the same way the Spirit (comes to us and) helps us in our weakness. We do not know what prayer to offer or how to offer it as we should, but the Spirit Himself (knows our need*

---

[71] 2 Corinthians 11:13 (NIV)
[72] 1 Corinthians 12:10 (NIV)
[73] 1 John 4:1 (NIV)
[74] 1 John 4:7 (NIV)
[75] 1 Corinthians 12:10 (NIV)
[76] 1 Corinthians 14:14 (AMP)

and at the right time) intercedes on our behalf with sighs and groanings too deep for words.

Romans 8:26 (AMP)

THE INTERPRETATION OF TONGUES

In the Greek the word *hermeneia* means 'the translation'. This is the supernatural ability to interpret a message in tongues spoken out to the church, so that the message in tongues can be understood by everybody in the church.

If anyone speaks in a tongue, two – or at the most three – should speak, one at a time and someone must interpret. If there is no interpreter, the speaker should keep quiet in the church and speak to himself and to God.

1 Corinthians 14:27-28 (NIV)

The Holy Spirit can give you the interpretation of your own tongue if praying alone.

Therefore let one who speaks in a tongue pray that he may (be gifted to) translate or explain (what he says). For if I pray in a tongue, my spirit prays, but my mind is unproductive (because it does not understand what my spirit is praying).

1 Corinthians 14:13-14 (AMP)

Sixteen Spiritual Gifts for Service

ADMINISTRATION

The Greek word *kubernesis* means 'to steer' or 'to guide'. This gift helps the church achieve God-inspired goals, by planning, organizing and supervising the execution of these plans.[77]

APOSTLE

In the Greek the word *apostolos* means 'to send forth'. The twelve disciples were the first apostles, but were unique in the sense that their commission was to establish the universal church and they had the

---

[77] See 1 Corinthians 12:28

authority to write scripture as they were inspired and directed by God. Paul said:

> *"Am I not an apostle? Have I not seen Jesus our Lord?"*
>
> 1 Corinthians 9:1 (NIV)

After Judas Iscariot betrayed Jesus Christ and then went out and hanged himself, the disciples had to select another apostle. They prayed to God for guidance to help them decide whether it should be Barsabbas or Matthias. After praying and casting lots they chose Matthias as he met a key criterion.

> *"For one of these must become a witness with us of his resurrection."*
>
> Acts 1:22 (NIV)

The role of those with the gift of apostleship today is to act as God's ambassador. Apostles are commissioned to start new ministries, plant churches and go to places where the gospel has not been preached.

> *"God has placed in the church first of all apostles."*
>
> 1 Corinthians 12:28 (NIV)

CELIBACY

This is the ability to voluntarily remain single so as to serve the Lord effectively without distraction, when high demands on one's time result in long periods away from home. This gift must be used in conjunction with other spiritual gifts as there is no merit in celibacy for its own sake.[78]

ENCOURAGING OR EXHORTATION

In the Greek the word *paraklesis* means 'calling to one's side'. This is the ability to come alongside someone with words of encouragement, comfort or advice to help them become effective in God's service, by building up their faith and providing encouragement when facing persecution or trials.

---

[78] See 1 Corinthians 7:7-8

EVANGELIST

In the Greek the word *euaggelistes* means literally 'a messenger of good news'. This is someone who preaches the gospel and has a heart to win unbelievers to the Lord.

> *So Christ himself gave the apostles, the prophets, the evangelists, the pastors and teachers, to equip his people for works of service so that the body of Christ may be built up.*
>
> Ephesians 4:11 (NIV)

GIVING

In the Greek the word *metadidomi* means 'to give over' or 'to share'. This is a person who is concerned for the needs of others and is willing to cheerfully and generously share their material possessions, money and time, without any expectation of receiving anything in return.[79]

HELPS

In the Greek, the word *antilepsis* means 'to partake or support'. 'Helps' provide support and assistance to others in the church which frees them up to use their ministry gifts.[80]

HOSPITALITY

The Greek word *philoxenos* means 'a love of strangers'. This is the ability to make welcome visitors and other members of the church into one's home. Hospitality involves helping those in need of food or accommodation.[81]

LEADING

The Greek word *proistemi* means 'to guide'. A leader is someone who has the responsibility of guiding other people in the church. Their style of leadership is to lead by example with wisdom and grace, demonstrating the 'fruit of the Spirit' by their actions and lifestyle. A

---

[79] See Romans 12:8
[80] See 1 Corinthians 12:28
[81] See 1 Peter 4:9-10

good leader will lead with sensitivity and motivate others to help achieve the ministry goals of the church.[82]

MARTYRDOM

The Greek word *paradidom* means 'to surrender'. A martyr will willingly sacrifice their life in the cause of serving Christ.[83]

MERCY

The Greek word *eleeo* means 'compassion'. This is caring sensitively for others who are suffering physically, mentally or emotionally, by being compassionate and behaving in ways that alleviate their distress.

If it is to show mercy, do it cheerfully.
Romans 12:8 (NIV)

MISSIONARY

This is the ability to minister in another culture, including a foreign country, or moving to work in a deprived inner-city area.[84]

PASTOR

The Greek word *poimen* means a 'shepherd, one who tends herds or flocks'. A pastor takes responsibility for the spiritual care and guidance of a group of believers or a church entrusted to their care.[85]

SERVING OR MINISTERING

In the Greek the word *diakonia* means 'deacon'. The role is to run errands and serve by providing practical help to those in need.[86]

TEACHING

The Greek word *didasko* means 'to give instruction'. A person with a teaching gift will instruct others in a systematic, logical way, explaining

---

[82] See Romans 12:8
[83] See 1 Corinthians 13:3
[84] See Ephesians 3:6-8
[85] See Ephesians 4:11
[86] See Romans 12:7

the word of God in a way that the person can understand and apply to their own life.

A gifted teacher has the unique ability to offer spiritual guidance by communicating knowledge and the doctrines of the faith.[87]

Voluntary Poverty

In the Greek the word *psomizo* means 'to supply with bits' or 'to nourish'. This is a person who has chosen to live at subsistence level, but not because of adverse circumstances. They place a low priority on their own comfort and convenience by willingly living on less in order to give more to helping others.[88]

The Gifts are Available Today

Some people believe the miraculous gifts being exercised in the Bible were needed for a specific purpose and for a limited time. Their reasoning is that once the early church had been established and the Bible had been completed, there was no further need of supernatural Holy Spirit gifts.

Those who hold this view argue that the following passage in Paul's letter to the church in Corinth makes this clear; but in fact the opposite is true.

> *Love never ends. As for prophecies, they will pass away; as for tongues, they will cease; as for knowledge, it will pass away. For we know in part and we prophesy in part, but when the perfect comes, the partial will pass away.*
>
> 1 Corinthians 13:8-10 (ESV)

Not an easy passage at first reading, but Paul points out the promise of eternal life for believers is something much more advanced than our present life on earth. He uses the example that when we grow up and become adults, we are capable of understanding things we could never comprehend as children. Paul says, although we cannot yet appreciate heaven in all its glory, when we go to heaven and are face to face with God, everything will fall into place. When that time comes, we will fully understand the true magnificence of the heavenly home God has prepared for us.

---

[87] See Romans 12:7
[88] See 1 Corinthians 13:3

> *For now (in this time of imperfection) we see in a mirror dimly (a blurred reflection, a riddle, an enigma), but then (when the time of perfection comes we will see reality) face to face. Now I know in part (just in fragments), but then I will know fully, just as I have been fully known (by God).*
>
> 1 Corinthians 13:12 (AMP)

We clearly won't need tongues, prophetic gifts or any miraculous spiritual gifts in heaven. God's punishment that followed the building of the Tower of Babel will be reversed. Originally all people had a common language, but that was until they angered God by attempting to build a tower in the plain of Shinar that reached to heaven.[89] God punished this rebellion by scattering everybody throughout the world and muddled up their common language so nobody could understand anybody else. This passage literally means that when the completeness of communication and knowledge comes, language barriers will not exist. In heaven we will be able to communicate and understand each other perfectly clearly. The Bible does not say how this will be achieved. It may be we will all speak the same universal language or, as some commentators believe, we will be able to speak all the languages of everyone else in the universe.

We do not know the answer to this question as many things in the Bible have not been revealed to us. We do know that with God all things are possible and this is not a problem for him; we have to take him at his word.

The Bible contains many scriptures that demonstrate to believers Jesus is the Messiah and will return again. When Jesus returned to heaven, he anointed his followers with his Holy Spirit to give them the power to witness and the strength to cope with being ridiculed and suffer persecution. The nine supernatural gifts, together with other spiritual gifts given to believers, are still in evidence today in churches and other ministries throughout the world.

Receiving the Baptism of the Holy Spirit

The primary purpose of all these spiritual gifts, available to those filled with the Holy Spirit, is to make us more like Jesus. A precondition is that we must surrender our whole nature to Jesus on a daily basis. We have to be sensitive to the promptings of the Holy Spirit, usually through

---

[89] See Genesis 11:1-9

Are Spiritual Gifts Relevant Today?

the exercising of our conscience, and allow him to change us and fill us with his love.

Supernatural spiritual gifts were given to those who were willing to seek in faith the fullness of the Holy Spirit. The Bible speaks of the Holy Spirit being 'poured out' without limit.[90]

> *[On the day of Pentecost,] all of them were filled with the Holy Spirit and began to speak in other tongues as the Spirit enabled them.*
>
> Acts 2:4 (NIV)

The prophet Joel said:

> *...in the last days, God says, I will pour out my Spirit on all people.*
>
> Acts 2:17 (NIV)

This outpouring of the Holy Spirit is frequently referred to in the Bible as the 'baptism of the Holy Spirit', which is total immersion in the Spirit of God, and for added emphasis the promise is repeated in each of the synoptic Gospels.

> *"He will baptize you (who truly repent) with the Holy Spirit and (you who remain unrepentant) with fire (judgment)."*
>
> Matthew 3:11; Mark 1:8; Luke 31:16 (AMP)

> *"When Paul began to speak, the Holy Spirit fell on them just as he did on us at the beginning (at Pentecost). Then I remembered the word of the Lord, how he used to say, 'John baptized with water, but you will be baptized with the Holy Spirit.'"*
>
> Acts 11:15-16 (AMP)

Points for Reflection

There are several potential barriers to receiving the baptism of the Holy Spirit. They can only be overcome by acknowledging them and asking the Lord for forgiveness.

- An unwillingness to trust God can be due to a lack of faith because some people who have bad life experiences blame God

---

[90] See John 3:34

and hold a grudge against God. This may be due to sad experiences where their self-esteem has been destroyed due to sexual or emotional abuse. This has left them feeling ashamed and guilty, even though they were the victim.

- An unwillingness by the individual to forgive people who have treated them unfairly and unjustly is a potential barrier because bitterness and possibly a desire for revenge is consuming the soul. Jesus said we have to forgive those who treat us badly and not remain bitter, if we want to receive his forgiveness and blessing.

"For if you forgive others their trespasses (their reckless and willful sins), your heavenly Father will also forgive you. But if you do not forgive others (nurturing your hurt and anger with the result that it interferes with your relationship with God), then your Father will not forgive your trespasses."

Matthew 6:14-15 (AMP)

- A believer who is apathetic and indifferent towards the Bible and its teaching will be unreceptive to the Holy Spirit speaking into their life. An unwillingness to follow the teaching contained in the Bible is a barrier to receiving the baptism of the Holy Spirit.

- Any involvement in the occult is a serious impediment to receiving the baptism of the Holy Spirit and needs to be renounced completely. Some seemingly harmless activities like consulting fortune-tellers or Tarot card readers or visiting psychics and using Ouija boards must be avoided. Regularly looking at horoscopes or listening to satanic music is also harmful and an obstacle to blessing.

  Anyone who worships pagan gods or is involved with astrology, or has any dealings with cults like the druids, witchcraft, Freemasonry, Luciferianism or is a member of the Theosophical Society, is engaged in activities which are forbidden by the Bible and grieve the Holy Spirit.

Let no one be found among you who sacrifices their son or daughter in the fire, who practices divination or sorcery, interprets omens, engages in witchcraft, or casts spells, or who is a spiritist or who consults the dead. Anyone who does these things is detestable to the LORD.

Deuteronomy 18:10-12 (NIV)

There is only one way to overcome these barriers and receive the power that comes with the baptism of the Holy Spirit. The answer is to renounce these harmful practices and seek God's cleansing and forgiveness.

A Personal Challenge

The challenge for each Christian is whether you are willing to let the Holy Spirit lead and guide you every day of your life. The apostle John, writing to a group of believers at Ephesus, stresses the importance of living a godly life and acting in a caring manner towards others; these are the outward signs of those who genuinely know God.

> *Little children (believers, dear ones) you are of God and you belong to Him and have (already) overcome them (the agents of the antichrist); because He who is in you is greater then he (Satan) who is in the world (of sinful mankind).*

1 John 4:4 (AMP)

The apostle Paul's message to the church at Thessalonica was one of encouragement: keep up the good work; you have been changed by the power of the Holy Spirit working in your lives.

> *It is clear to us, friends, that God not only loves you very much but also has put his hand on you for something special. When the message we preached came to you, it wasn't just words. Something happened in you. The Holy Spirit put steel in your convictions.*

1 Thessalonians 1:4-6 (MSG)

Difficult Questions for Christians

Questions

Why is the Bible's view of our gifts and talents different from the world's view?

Is the fruit of the Spirit more important than the gifts of the Spirit, and if so, why?

Why are only some of the gifts of the Spirit being exercised in some churches and none in others?

Why were all the gifts of the Spirit active in the early church but there is less evidence of them being exercised in the twenty-first century church today?

Which gifts of the Spirit are not active in the church today?

What would the perfect church in terms of fruit and gifts look like? Is it achievable?

CHAPTER SIX

Should I Tithe if I Pay Tax?

Introduction

The Hebrew word *ma'aser* means 'tithe', which is giving one-tenth of one's income and goods for religious purposes. Tithing was a common practice in the Old Testament and the Israelites were required to tithe. Tithing is specifically mentioned in the Bible as early as the book of Genesis.

> *And Abraham gave him (King Melchizedek) one-tenth of everything.*
>
> *Genesis 14:20 (NRSV)*

Jacob tithed his property to God after his vision at Luz.

> *'If God will be with me, and will keep me in this way that I go, and will give me bread to eat and clothing to wear so that I come to my father's house again in peace, then the LORD shall be my God ... and of all of that you give me I will surely give one-tenth to you.'*
>
> *Genesis 28:20-22 (NRSV)*

With the coming of Mosaic law, three tithes were prescribed, which altogether amounted to 23% of the Hebrew people's income. The first tithe was for the Levites and was a yearly tithe.[91] The second tithe was for the individual and his household to cover expenses at the national feasts, so there would be no excuse for not going.[92] The third tithe was for the Levites, the strangers, fatherless and widows. It was a special tithe

---

[91] See Deuteronomy 14:27
[92] See Deuteronomy 14:24

for the poor, a charity tithe to relieve suffering of poor neighbours.[93] The additional tithe for the Levites was given every third year because they owned no land and had no other means of support.

> *At the end of every three years, bring all the tithe of that year's produce and store it in your towns, so that the Levites (who have no allotment or inheritance of their own) and the foreigners, the fatherless and the widows of your towns may come and eat and be satisfied, and God may bless you in all the work of your hands.*
>
> Deuteronomy 14:28-29 (NIV)

In reality these were not freewill offerings as they were used to finance the government of the day in the same way that we are expected to pay our taxes.

> *This is also why you pay taxes, for the authorities are God's servants, who give their full time to governing. Give to everyone what you owe them: If you owe taxes, pay taxes.*
>
> Romans 13:6-7 (NIV)

The Jews were required to make periodic sin offerings from their cattle and other animals in addition to tithing. The Hebrew word *minhah* means 'to make an offering' which is a voluntary gift to the church and is made in addition to the tithe required under Mosaic law.

Attitude to Giving

The standard set out in the New Testament was arguably more demanding than under the Mosaic law. Whilst it abolished the legal requirement to give ten per cent of one's income to the Levites,[94] the emphasis was now on the attitude of the person giving – to give generously from a grateful heart.

> *Remember this: Whoever sows sparingly will also reap sparingly, and whoever sows generously will also reap generously. Each of you should give as you have decided in your heart to give, not reluctantly or under compulsion, for God loves a cheerful giver. And God is able to bless you*

---

[93] See Deuteronomy 14:28-29
[94] See Numbers 18:24

abundantly, so that in all things at all times, having all that you need, you will abound in every good work.

2 Corinthians 9:6-8 (NIV)

When Jesus told the parable of the Good Samaritan,[95] one of the points he made was that generous people give more than financial resources; they give of their time and show hospitality to those who are in need or vulnerable or less fortunate than themselves.

Do not neglect to do good and to share what you have, for such sacrifices are pleasing to God.

Hebrews 13:16 (ESV)

Regular Giving

The Apostle Paul gives clear guidance to believers that our giving should be regular and systematic. He tells them to set aside a set amount of their income every Sunday on the basis of how well they have been financially blessed.

On the first day of every week, each of you is to put something aside and store it up, as he may prosper, so that there will be no collecting when I come.

1 Corinthians 16:2 (ESV)

The reason was to enable the church to budget effectively and so there was no need to have special collections when Paul came to stay. He wanted to ensure that his time with the church was used for preaching and teaching and not wasted raising money to support him.

What does the Bible Say About Tithing in the Old Testament?

We have seen that although tithing was obligatory in the Old Testament, the Israelites were being dishonest in making their tithes and offerings to God. God spoke to the nation of Israel through his prophet Malachi (his name means 'my messenger') who told them God was very angry they had neglected to fully tithe. They had cheated God by bringing blind, lame and sick animals to the temple as sacrifices instead of perfect animals as was required.

---

[95] See Luke 10:30-37

In the past God had punished them for their disobedience by allowing drought, crop failure and pestilence and disease to affect their crops. Given they were a farming nation, crops were essential for their survival and prosperity.

Malachi told them the solution was to repent and bring the full tithe into the temple warehouse. Once the tithes and offerings had been collected, they were distributed to the priests and Levites in order to provide for their families and for sacrificial purposes.

> *Will anyone rob God? Yet you are robbing me! But you say, "How are we robbing you?" In your tithes and offerings! You are cursed with a curse, for you are robbing me – the whole nation of you! Bring the full tithe into the storehouse, so that there may be food in my house, and thus put me to the test, says the LORD of hosts; see if I will not open the windows of heaven for you and pour down for you an overflowing blessing.*
>
> Malachi 3:8-12 (NRSV)

This passage is often misinterpreted as a promise to all Christians that tithing brings material prosperity. However, this is not the modern equivalent of a 'prosperity gospel'; this was God telling the Israelites to stop being disobedient and he would continue to bless them as in the past. The Israelites were guilty, as are some Christians today, of claiming the promises of God but failing to accept the obligations of obeying God's commandments. It is important to appreciate God's promises are not unconditional but are dependent on following him obediently.

What does the Bible Say About Tithing in the New Testament?

There is a view amongst some Christians today that tithing, which was obligatory in Old Testament days, doesn't apply nowadays as we are under 'the law of grace'. The Apostle Paul acknowledges that many Old Testament practices are no longer compulsory; we no longer need to sacrifice animals, and men are no longer required to be circumcised.[96] Instead Paul urges us to find out what is the will of God, what is the right thing to do.

---

[96] See Romans 2:29

Should I Tithe if I Pay Tax?

> *Jesus said, "Do not think that I have come to abolish the law or the prophets: I have come not to abolish but to fulfill. For I tell you, until heaven and earth pass away, not one letter, not one stroke of a letter, will pass from the law until all is accomplished."*
>
> *Matthew 5:17-18 (NRSV)*

There are few references in the New Testament to tithing but Jesus was quick to condemn the Pharisees for their double standards.

> *"Woe to you, scribes and Pharisees, hypocrites! For you tithe mint, dill, (a sweet-smelling herb of the parsley family) and cumin (seeds of a similar plant used as a spice) and have neglected the weightier matters of the law: justice and mercy and faith. It is these you ought to have practiced without neglecting the others."*
>
> *Matthew 23:23 (NRSV)*

In Dake's Annotated Reference Bible, he states:

> *Since Christ sanctioned tithing then it should be practised. His teachings were not to confirm the law for a few days and then be abolished, they were to take the place of the law.*

Some scholars argue that Jesus was saying they should continue to tithe, but they were not to neglect more important matters.

> *Jesus looked up and saw rich people putting their gifts into the treasury; he also saw a poor widow put in two small copper coins. He said, "Truly I tell you, this poor widow has put in more than all of them, for all of them have contributed out of their abundance, but she out of her poverty has put in all she had to live on."*
>
> *Luke 21:1-4 (NRSV)*

Jesus measured the widow's giving not by the value of what she gave but by what she had left! This is the new concept of giving. The poor widow who gave her all gave more than the others who gave a very small part of their all. In this context the issue of making tithes and offerings takes on a new significance. We are encouraged to revise our giving when our circumstances improve, such as on receipt of a pay rise or a legacy.

> *Honor the LORD with your wealth and with the firstfruits of all your produce; then your barns will be filled with plenty, and your vats will be bursting with wine.*
>
> Proverbs 3:9-10 (ESV)

The apostle Paul raises the idea that giving generously will result in material blessing when writing to the church in Corinth. Paul says our aim should be primarily to be a blessing to others, particularly the poor. This could take the form of supporting the outreach work of your church if it runs a food bank or by supporting the work of *bona fide* Christian charities.

The late Selwyn Hughes was an evangelical preacher, teacher and minister. He considered these verses in Proverbs to be some of the most profound verses on the biblical principle of giving generously and in the right spirit.

> *One man gives freely, yet gains even more; another withholds unduly, but comes to poverty. A generous person will prosper; whoever refreshes others will be refreshed.*
>
> Proverbs 11:24-25 (NIV)

Trusting the Church With Your Tithes

There is no greater responsibility than becoming a leader in the church of Jesus Christ. The apostle Paul, writing to Timothy in Ephesus, sets out the high standard of personal and spiritual qualities that are necessary to serve in a leadership role in the church. He lists the essential qualifications, which can be summarized as commitment, conviction, competency, character and integrity.[97]

> *Let the elders who rule well be considered worthy of double honor especially those who labor in preaching and teaching: for the scripture says, "You shall not muzzle an ox while it is treading out the grain," and, "The laborer deserves to be paid."*
>
> 1 Timothy 5:17-18 (NRSV)

Good church leaders will be mindful of the importance of being good stewards of the tithes and offerings received from church members.

---

[97] See 1 Timothy 3:1-13

Effective stewardship can be ensured by considering the following suggestions:

- Ensure that those with sufficient income to pay income tax are signing a declaration so that Gift Aid is claimed, thus adding 25% to the value of their planned giving in the UK.

- Convene regular church meetings, where financial matters are discussed openly.

- Although church members are to respect the leaders and submit to their authority,[98] they have a responsibility to examine the church accounts periodically and be satisfied good stewardship is being exercised.

- The church leadership team must comprise individuals who take their responsibilities seriously and are willing to be accountable to the church membership for managing the Lord's tithes and offerings prudently. They are not autonomous but are ultimately accountable to God for how they discharge their responsibilities.

- Issues of trust can arise where there is evidence of mismanagement or even corruption within the church leadership team. Whilst this should be challenged, in such circumstances the individual may have no alternative other than to consider finding a new church.

Points for Reflection

Making regular tithes and offerings to the church is no substitute for salvation. Salvation is available to all who believe Jesus was the Son of God who came to earth to die on the cross for our sins and was gloriously raised from the dead. It is available to everyone who repents of their sins and accepts Jesus Christ as their personal Saviour.

> *For by grace you have been saved through faith; it is not of yourselves, it is the gift of God; not as a result of works, so that no one may boast.*
>
> *Ephesians 2:8-9 (ESV)*

---

[98] See Hebrews 13:7

Salvation has no bearing on how well we live our lives and how generous we are to those less fortunate than ourselves. The apostle Paul makes it very clear.

For all have sinned and come short of the glory of God.
Romans 3:23 (NIV)

Personal Challenge

A final thought from the late Billy Graham about tithing:

We have found in our home that God's blessing upon the nine-tenths, when we tithe, helps it to go further.

Do not store up for yourselves treasures on earth, where moth and rust consume and where thieves break in and steal; but store up for yourselves treasure in heaven, where neither moth nor rust consumes and where thieves do not break in. For where your treasure is, there your heart will be also.
Matthew 6:19-21 (NRSV)

Questions

Are we thankful to God for blessing our families and us materially?

How should we determine the level of our giving to the Lord's work?

What advice would you give about tithing to someone who is in substantial debt?

How does tithing apply to someone who is married to an unbeliever?

How should a member handle issues where the Lord's tithes and offerings are being wasted or used inappropriately by the pastor and church leadership?

How should a church that is financially secure invest its money?

Chapter Seven

Why is Predestination Such a Dilemma?

Introduction

The Greek word *proorizo* means 'to determine beforehand or to decide ahead of time'. Predestination means that God knows everything that will happen in the future. The Cambridge Dictionary defines predestination as 'the belief that people have no control over events because these things are controlled by God or by fate'. The issue of predestination is one of those conundrums that Christians find difficult to unravel. This is not surprising, as it has been the subject of much debate amongst scholars since the third century!

God's Perspective

God is holy and sin cannot live alongside a perfect God. Sin entered the world when Adam and Eve disobeyed God's express instructions and surrendered to temptation by Satan, a fallen angel, and this allowed sin to enter the world. Sin created an immense gulf between God and mankind. God is a God of love. He created the world and all of us, and he does not wish for anyone to be separated from him for all eternity.

How did God choose who would become sons of God and who would be condemned to eternal separation from him? Why did God give us all free will to make decisions for ourselves? Presumably, he didn't want us to be robots that just carried out his commands; he wanted to have a proper, real and meaningful relationship with us.

God wants us to freely choose to love and serve him, but as God has unlimited power and knowledge, he knows before we do whether we are going to choose to serve him.

The Theological Dilemma

John Calvin (1509-1564) was a Protestant French theologian who believed predestination meant God had predestined some people for salvation (unconditional election) and some for condemnation (reprobation) which is a result of allowing the sins of the individual to condemn them. John Calvin defines predestination as "the eternal decree of God, by which he determined with himself whatever he wished to happen with regard to every man. Not all are created on equal terms, but some are preordained to eternal life, others to eternal damnation: and accordingly, as each has been created for one or other of these ends, we say he has been predestined to life or death." John Calvin thought people who were saved could never lose their salvation and the notion of double predestination is the doctrine that God actively decrees damnation as well as salvation.

St Augustine of Hippo (AD 354 - AD 430) was a Catholic Bishop, theologian and prolific writer who believed all events that occur are the will of God. This included the eternal destiny of the human soul, based on God's foreknowledge of each person and what he had determined from the beginning of time, in his grace; who he would save and who he would not, regardless of their faith, love or merit, or lack of merit. St Augustine of Hippo laid the foundation for much of later Catholic teaching on predestination and the following is a quotation from his book *On Grace and Free Will*:

> *God promised not from the power of our will but from his own predestination. For he promised what He Himself would do, not what men would do. Because, although men do those good things that pertain to God's worship, He Himself makes them do what he has commanded; it is not they that cause Him to do what He has promised. Otherwise the fulfillment of God's promises would not be in the power of God, but that of men.*

The Lutherans hold to 'unconditional election' in respect of salvation, but do not believe that certain people are predestined to salvation. They believe that salvation is predestined for those who seek God. Lutherans do not believe in the concept of predestination to damnation but teach that eternal damnation is the result of the unbeliever's sins, their rejection of the forgiveness of sins and of unbelief.

Scholars over the centuries have debated the concept of predestination, but the dilemma is, does God ultimately make the decision about choosing who will receive salvation or is it the individual exercising their free will?

God's Foreknowledge

The Greek word *proorizo* means 'to pre-establish boundaries or limits'. The Greek word *eklektos* means 'selected or chosen' and can refer to a nation such as Israel or to an individual known as 'the elect of God'.

God had foreknowledge about each and every single person on this planet.

> *Before I formed you in the womb I knew you, and before you were born I consecrated you; I appointed you to be a prophet to the nations.*
>
> *Jeremiah 1:5 (NRSV)*

> *For I know the plans I have for you, declares the LORD, plans for your welfare and not for evil, to give you a future and a hope.*
>
> *Jeremiah 29:11 (ESV)*

God's foreknowledge is not limited to how each of us will live our lives. God knew how history would unfold and he knows how 'end times' events will develop and the final outcome. The Bible contains many prophecies that have already been fulfilled, but there are many prophecies about future events yet to occur.

The signs and sequence of events that point to the second coming of Jesus Christ are recorded by the apostle John in the book of Revelation. He states, God knew who would accept the gift of salvation, even before the world had been created, and their names have already been written in the Book of Life.

> *All the inhabitants of the earth will fall down and worship him, everyone whose name has not been written since the foundation of the world in the Book of Life of the Lamb who was slain (as a willing sacrifice).*
>
> *Revelation 13:8 (AMP)*

Adoption into God's Family

God's plan was gracious and ambitious: he wants everyone to accept the gift of salvation, as this is the only way to become his sons and daughters for eternity.

> *'But I say to you, "Love your enemies and pray for those who persecute you, so that you may be children of your Father in Heaven."'*
>
> *Matthew 5:45 (NRSV)*

The apostle Paul makes it plain that as believers we become the children of God and he carefully selected us to become adopted into his family. The parallel with adoption is not accidental; all adopted children in the natural are special because they are not randomly conceived but have been chosen to become part of a family.

> *Long, long ago, he decided to adopt us into his family through Jesus Christ.*
>
> *Ephesians 1:5 (MSG)*

Adopted children have the same legal rights as natural children so when God adopts us into his family we become joint heirs with his son Jesus Christ.

> *For all who are led by the Spirit of God are children of God. For you did not receive a spirit of slavery to fall back into fear, but you have received a spirit of adoption. When we cry 'Abba! Father!' it is that very Spirit bearing witness with our Spirit that we are children of God, and if children, then heirs, heirs of God and joint heirs with Christ.*
>
> *Romans 8:14-17 (NRSV)*

Saved by Grace

Grace is the free and undeserved gift from God in which he invites us to become his children and become adopted into his heavenly family. The offer is unconditional; all we have to do is exercise our free will and believe that Jesus Christ is the son of God and accept through faith the gift of salvation.

> *For by grace you have been saved through faith. And this is not of your own doing, it is the gift of God, not a result of works, so that no one may boast.*
>
> Ephesians 2:8-9 (ESV)

There is no other way to be saved from the consequences of sin in our lives. Jesus said that he was the only way we could be saved:

> *"I am the way and the truth and the life. No one comes to the Father except through me."*
>
> John 14:6 (NIV)

> *"And there is salvation in no one else; for there is no other name under heaven that has been given among men by which we must be saved (for God has provided the world no alternative for salvation)."*
>
> Acts 4:12 (AMP)

The Greek word *dikaion* means 'righteous' and no matter how hard we try to do good in our lives, we can never be righteous in the sight of God.

> *For the wages of sin is death, but the free gift of God is eternal life in Christ Jesus our Lord.*
>
> Romans 6:23 (ESV)

Is Evangelism Necessary?

God calls Christians to be active about sharing their faith because this gives praise to God, encourages faith in others and is consistent with the biblical view that we are God's ambassadors on earth to be witnesses to the unsaved.

> *And he said to them, 'Go into all the world and proclaim the good news to the whole creation.'*
>
> Mark 16:15 (NRSV)

> *"Therefore go and make disciples of all nations, baptizing them in the name of the Father and of the Son and of the Holy Spirit, and teaching them to obey everything I have commanded you."*
>
> Matthew 28:19 (NIV)

This was not just a commandment Jesus gave to his disciples before he ascended into heaven. His instruction to share the good news was accompanied by providing his followers with the power to witness through the gift of his Holy Spirit.

> *The gifts he (Jesus Christ) gave were that some would be apostles, some prophets, some evangelists, some pastors and teachers, to equip the saints for the work of ministry, for building up the body of Christ, until all of us come to the unity of the faith and of the knowledge of the Son of God, to maturity to the full stature of Christ.*
>
> Ephesians 4:11-13 (NRSV)

The apostle Paul fervently believed his preaching and his prayers could make a difference. He believed the lost could become believers by hearing the good news of Jesus Christ.

> *Brothers and sisters, my heart's desire and prayer to God for them is that they may be saved.*
>
> Romans 10:1 (ESV)

> *...I have voluntarily become a servant to any and all in order to reach a wide range of people: religious, nonreligious, meticulous moralists, loose-living immoralists, the defeated, the demoralized – whoever. I didn't take on their way of life. I kept my bearings in Christ – but I entered their world and tried to experience things from their point of view. I've become just about every kind of servant there is in my attempts to lead those I meet into a God-saved life. I did all this because of the Message.*
>
> 1 Corinthians 9:19-23 (MSG)

What the Bible Says About Our Future

The Bible teaches that God clearly predestined that many people would accept the gift of salvation and become full members of his family.

> *We know that all things work together for good for those who love God who are called according to his purpose. For those who he foreknew he also predestined to be conformed to the image of his Son, in order that he might be the firstborn within a large family. And those whom he predestined he also called;*

> *and those whom he called he also justified; and those whom he justified he also glorified.*
>
> Romans 8:28-30 (NRSV)

> *He predestined us to be adopted as his sons through Jesus Christ, in accordance with his pleasure and will.*
>
> Ephesians 1:5 (ESV)

God's plan is for us to have a glorious eternal future with him in heaven. However, he realized that once sin had come into the world our lives on earth would be full of troubles and heartache, which was not his original plan.

God wants us to put our trust in him and he will not be deflected from his plan to give us a life full of blessing and fulfilment.

> *For surely I know the plans I have for you, says the LORD, plans for your welfare and not for harm, to give you a future with hope.*
>
> Jeremiah 29:11 (NRSV)

He compares our life as believers to taking part in a race, a marathon. Taking part in a marathon is very arduous and exhausting. It requires fitness training and planning to be a successful marathon runner. There are obstacles to overcome, kerbstones and cobbled streets to negotiate, as well as setbacks caused by injuries, so it requires perseverance. Marathon runners talk of 'hitting the wall' at about the twenty-mile mark; this is when the runner's glycogen (stored energy) in the muscles becomes depleted, forcing them to slow down. Following the training schedule helps the runner to reduce these problems, but in the end the desire to complete the race is the spur to keep pressing on through the pain barrier. It is not how we start, it is how we finish that is important.

> *Keep your eyes on Jesus, who both began and finished this race we're in. Study how he did it. Because he never lost sight of where he was headed – that exhilarating finish in and with God – he could put up with anything along the way: cross, shame, whatever. And now he's there, in the place of honour, right alongside God. When you find yourselves flagging in your faith, go over that story again, item by item, that long*

litany of hostility he ploughed through. That will shoot adrenaline into your souls!

Hebrews 12:2 (MSG)

The thought that God is the author of all history and we are 'his story' reminds us that the author always knows how the story ends, before the reader!

Points for Reflection

We cannot fathom or hope to comprehend how awesome God's almighty power is.

It is frankly mind-boggling that God created this vast universe. According to scientists, the Andromeda Galaxy, our nearest neighbouring galaxy, is 2.5 million light years away with a width of 220,000 light years. The Rosette Nebula is five thousand light years away with a width of 130 light years. It has been calculated that a space shuttle travelling at five miles a second would take 37,200 years to travel just one light year, which is 5.8786×10^{12} miles, or approximately six trillion miles away!

God created the whole universe with its billions of stars, including our earthly home with all its beauty and resources. God is all-knowing, all-seeing and has always existed and always will be. His power and knowledge are unlimited and we cannot hope with our finite minds to begin to understand that.

God loves his creation, but he particularly loved the human race which he created in his own image. Once sin came into the world our true nature became apparent: we are a selfish, immoral, godless and rebellious people.

God so loved the world that he gave his one and only Son, that whoever believes in him shall not perish but have eternal life.

John 3:16 (NIV)

When we accept Jesus Christ as our personal Saviour, through his grace, we become adopted into his family as God's children. That is the measure of his love and plan for our lives if we truly repent of our sins and accept his salvation.

We cannot place limits on God's almighty power (omnipotence), his vast and immeasurable knowledge (omniscience) and comprehend the fact he is everywhere at the same time (omnipresence). It is impossible for us to comprehend the splendour and magnificence of God who knows the beginning from the end of time. We should not be surprised to learn that God knows everything about us; even before we were born he knew us, and he knows our future and every decision we will make in our lives. When we choose to accept the gift of salvation, God becomes our Father, our Protector, our Saviour, and nothing can ever come between us.

A Personal Challenge

Our examination of this challenging issue should encourage us to be grateful that we are a chosen people. It should inspire us to resolve to serve our Lord through the power of his Holy Spirit.

> *Trust in the LORD with all your heart and lean not on your own understanding; in all your ways submit to him, and he will make your paths straight.*
>
> *Proverbs 3:5-6 (NIV)*

Questions

Is predestination unfair to those who have not been given the opportunity to repent and turn to Jesus Christ?

_____

_____

If we are predestined to be children of God for eternity, does it matter how I live my life on this earth?

_____

_____

Why are we called to evangelize when God has decided beforehand who will be saved?

_____

_____

Can you lose your salvation once you have been predestined to be saved?

_____

_____

How should we be living our lives as Christians now that we have accepted, through his grace, the gift of salvation?

_____

_____

Is the concept of predestination another demonstration of God's omnipotence and our limited ability to understand the mind of God?

_____

_____

Chapter Eight

Can God Bless Gay Marriages?

Introduction

LGBT stands for Lesbian, Gay, Bisexual, Transgender persons, but since 1996 the 'Q' has been added for those who are questioning their identity or who identify as Queer. Although 'queer' is an umbrella term for those with same-sex desires, it is also used as a term of abuse. In the last few years the established LGBT abbreviation has acquired a few extra letters: LGBTQIA. The 'I' represents Inter-sex and the 'A' represents those who are Asexual or Allied.

A 'lesbian' is a female who is attracted to other females, whereas the term 'gay' is normally used to refer to homosexual men but can also include females.

A 'bisexual' person is attracted to both sexes and can be a man or a woman. The gender of a 'transgender' person is fluid and they move between genders.

A 'transsexual' person is someone who wants to live as a member of the opposite sex and receives sex reassignment surgery (SRS) to make their sexual characteristics match their gender identity. Individuals who have completed SRS are sometimes referred to as trans sexed.

Current Research Findings

The first official attempt to quantify the number of LGTB persons was conducted by Treasury actuaries in 2005 when asked to analyse the financial implications of the Civil Partnership Act 2004. They estimated there were 3.6 million gay and lesbian people in the UK.

A survey conducted by the Office for National Statistics (ONS) found the number of lesbian, gay or bisexual persons had increased from 1.7% in 2015 to 2% of the population by 2016, to a total of one million persons, which the ONS described as a 'statistically significant increase'.

In July 2017 the government launched a 'national LGBT survey' which they asked LGBT people to complete and they received over 108,100 valid responses from persons over the age of sixteen. The government equalities office published the results in July 2018 and the findings were as follows:

About 6 out of 10 respondents were gay or lesbian, about a quarter of the respondents were bisexual, about 1 in 8 respondents were transgender, and about 1 in every 15 respondents were non-binary.

A person who is 'non-binary' is someone who does not think of themselves as male or female.

Evidence suggests that people identifying as LGTB are at a higher risk of experiencing a range of mental health problems such as depression, suicidal thoughts, self-harm, alcohol and substance misuse. According to the Mental Health Foundation this can be attributable to a range of factors such as discrimination, isolation, homophobia and hate crime.

A total of 24% of the LGTB respondents had accessed mental health services in the previous twelve months and 27% had accessed sexual health services in the same period.

The NHS Gender Identity Development Service supports children, mainly girls, experiencing 'difficulties in the development of their gender identity'. The number of referrals has risen from 97 in 2009/10 to a total of 2,519 in 2017/18. The NHS reports that the fourteen Gender Identity Clinics (GICs) are struggling to cope.

The American Psychological Association, formed in 1975, are taking the lead in removing the stigma of mental illness that has long been associated with lesbian, gay and bi-sexual orientations. They have published their findings in a pamphlet titled *Sexual Orientation and Homosexuality* and state:

There is no consensus among scientists about the exact reasons that an individual develops a heterosexual, bisexual, gay or lesbian orientation. Although much research has examined the possible genetic, hormonal, developmental, social and cultural influences on sexual orientation, no findings have emerged that permit scientists to conclude that sexual orientation is determined by any particular factor or factors.

God's Idea Was Marriage

It is important to put the subject of sexual relationships in the context of what God had in mind when he created man and women. When God created man he planned to provide him with a companion because he realized the importance of having a personal relationship with another human being.

> *God put the man into a deep sleep. As he slept he removed one of his ribs and replaced it with flesh. God then used the rib that he had taken from the Man to make Woman and presented her to the Man.*
> *Genesis 2:21-23 (MSG)*

It was God's intention that this marital relationship would be a lifelong monogamous relationship in which 'a man leaves his father and mother and is united to his wife, and they become one flesh'[99].

Having created this special relationship, God invented sex so they could have a family and in time populate the earth with millions of human beings.

> *God blessed them, and said to them, "Be fruitful and increase in number; fill the earth and subdue it."*
> *Genesis 1:28 (NIV)*

It is clear from the Bible that sexual relationships are to be conducted within the framework of a loving relationship, where children can be conceived and brought up within a stable home with two parents, who are male and female.

> *It is good for a man to have a wife, and for a woman to have a husband. Sexual drives are strong, but marriage is strong enough to contain them and provide for a balanced and fulfilling sexual life in a world of sexual disorder.*
> *1 Corinthians 7:2-3 (MSG)*

Jesus warned that marriage is not for everyone and recognized that sustaining a lifelong relationship calls for maturity, love and resilience to weather the storms of life and the pressure that raising children places on a relationship.

---

[99] Genesis 2:24 (NIV)

> *Jesus said, "Not everyone is mature enough to live a married life. It requires a certain aptitude and grace. Marriage is not for everyone."*
>
> Matthew 19:11-12 (MSG)

Divorce and Adultery

God recognized that human beings are sinful and for various reasons are unable to sustain the marital relationship as intended. Jesus taught that divorce is contrary to God's plan, but acknowledged that Moses was reluctantly obliged to make arrangements for couples who could no longer tolerate living together.

> *Moses permitted you to divorce your wives because your hearts were hard. But it was not this way from the beginning. I tell you that anyone who divorces his wife, except for sexual immorality, and marries another woman commits adultery.*
>
> Matthew 19:8-9 (NIV)

'You shall not commit adultery'[100] is one of the Ten Commandments and is mentioned fifty-two times in the Bible including all four Gospels and ten other books. Adultery occurs when a married person has sexual relations with someone other than their wife.

The Ten Commandments are unequivocal; married persons are not to break their sacred lifelong vows and commit adultery.

> *He who commits adultery lacks sense; he who does it destroys himself.*
>
> Proverbs 6:32 (ESV)

Jesus states that even when a marital relationship has broken down and a couple divorce, it is not acceptable to remarry if the original marriage partner is still alive, unless they have committed adultery.

> *Everyone who divorces his wife and marries another commits adultery, and he who marries a woman divorced from her husband commits adultery.*
>
> Luke 16:18 (ESV)

The Bible teaches that marriage is an exclusive loving and sexual relationship between a husband and wife. There are no circumstances

---

[100] Exodus 21:14 (NIV)

where sex with another person is acceptable, even if one party, for whatever reason, is unable to fulfil the sexual needs of their spouse. Although adultery is *grounds* for divorce, there is no *requirement* to divorce. If a couple are reconciled and continue to live together and resume sexual relations, that is not a sin. God will forgive the sin of adultery if the guilty party sincerely repents.

> *For I will be merciful and gracious toward their wickedness, and I will remember their sins no more.*
>
> Hebrews 8:12 (AMP)

LGBT and Homosexuality

Two words in the Greek are used to describe homosexuality: *malakoi*, which means 'moral weakness' and *arsenokoitai*, which comprises two Greek words, *arse* meaning 'men' and *nokoitai* meaning 'bed'; when put together it means 'men who bed other men'. A homosexual person is sexually attracted to and engages in sexual activity with a person of his or her own sex. In essence, all lesbian, gay, bisexual and transgender persons who are in a sexual relationship are 'homosexual'.

The Bible makes it very clear that sex outside a marital relationship is unacceptable to God and will result in judgement.

> *Do not be deceived: Neither the sexually immoral nor idolaters nor adulterers nor men who have sex with men nor thieves nor the greedy nor drunkards, nor slanderers nor swindlers will inherit the kingdom of God.*
>
> 1 Corinthians 6:9-10 (NIV)

When human beings disobey God and ignore God's standards of behaviour, this inevitably leads to all kinds of sinful behaviour.

> *Refusing to know God, they soon didn't know how to be human either – women didn't know how to be women, men didn't know how to be men. Sexually confused, they abused and defiled one another, women with women, men with men; all lust, and no love.*
>
> Romans 1:26-27 (MSG)

The Bible demonstrates that all homosexual activity is forbidden rather than certain expressions of it, as it violates God's standards.

Fornication

The Greek word *porneia* means 'fornication', which is sex between people who are unmarried. Other interpretations of *porneia* are whoredom, or idolatry connected with prostitution and the worship of fertility gods.

One of the reasons God destroyed the cities of Sodom and Gomorrah was because of the widespread prevalence of homosexuality and depravity which the inhabitants of both cities indulged in, hence the association with the word sodomy. The male inhabitants were so corrupt they wanted to perform homosexual gang rape on the two angels who came in human form to warn Lot that God was going to destroy the cities because of their very 'grave'[101] sins.

> ...just as Sodom and Gomorrah and the surrounding cities, which likewise indulged in sexual immorality and pursued unnatural desire, serve as an example by undergoing a punishment of eternal fire.
>
> Jude 1:7 (ESV).

It is clear that homosexuality is fornication and will result in punishment by God as will other perverted acts.

Gender Dysphoria

The National Health Service describes gender dysphoria as a distressing condition in which a person feels there is an emotional and psychological identity mismatch between their biological sex and gender identity. The Equality and Human Rights Commission found in 2012 that 1% of the population was gender variant. There are other rare gender dysphoria conditions, such as congenital adrenal hyperplasia (CAH), in which a high level of male hormones in a female foetus creates some concern as to whether the baby is male when she is born.

Other rare medical conditions include a person who is a 'hermaphrodite' – born either with the genitalia of both sexes or with ambiguous genitalia.

---

[101] Genesis 18:20 (NRSV)

Persons who suffer with gender dysphoria or other rare conditions are often confused and distressed individuals who are emotionally and spiritually damaged.

What the Bible Says About Sexual Relationships

It is important to appreciate what the Bible describes as unacceptable sexual behaviour. God takes immoral behaviour very seriously and the book of Leviticus states that the penalty is 'death'. The Bible is emphatic: sexual relationships are only to take place within a marital relationship.

After God spoke to Moses, he spelt out the rules of sexual behaviour to the Israelites in considerable detail in Leviticus 18. These included not to have sex with close relatives[102] or with a woman during her monthly period.[103] Another command was:

> *Don't have sex with an animal and violate yourself by it. A woman must not have sex with an animal. That is perverse. Don't pollute yourself in any of these ways.*
>
> Leviticus 18:23 (MSG)

The Bible is clear: all forms of fornication and deviant behaviour are abhorrent to God including homosexuality and cross-dressing.

> *If a man has sex with a man as one does with a woman, both of them have done what is abhorrent.*
>
> Leviticus 20:13 (MSG)

Cross-dressing is also forbidden as it is an attempt to deceive, by purporting to be a member of the opposite sex.

> *A woman shall not wear men's clothing, nor a man wear a women's clothing, for the LORD your God detests anyone who does this.*
>
> Deuteronomy 22:5 (NIV)

We describe a man who enjoys dressing up in woman's clothing as a 'transvestite'. This verse is not intended to be offering fashion advice, as there is no biblical reason why women should not wear slacks or men wear kilts. It is the motive behind any attempt to deceive someone else about their gender which is being questioned. The modern-day equivalent

---

[102] See Leviticus 18:6
[103] See Leviticus 18:19

would be a man or woman purporting to be of the opposite sex on an online forum or Internet chat room; invariably, the motives are highly suspect.

> *You are to be holy to me because I, the LORD, am holy, and I have set you apart from the nations to be my own.*
>
> Leviticus 20:26 (NIV)

Be Good Role Models

God wants believers to celebrate their physical differences. Men are encouraged to act as men and women to act as women. The apostle Paul emphasizes the importance of women acting as good role models.

> *Likewise tell the older women to be reverent in behavior, not to be slanderers or slaves to drink, they are to teach what is good, so that they may encourage the young women to love their husbands, to love their children, to be self-controlled, chaste, good managers of the household, kind, being submissive to their husbands.*
>
> Titus 2:3-5 (NRSV)

When the apostle Paul writes to Titus he makes it clear how mature women should conduct themselves and the type of role models they should be offering to the younger women. In a similarly forthright manner he tells the men to act as men and set high standards and act as good role models for the younger men. Paul clearly appreciated the distinct roles that God had prescribed for men and women, based primarily on their gender.

> *Tell the older men to be temperate, serious, prudent, and sound in faith, in love, and in endurance. Urge the young men to be self-controlled. Show yourself in all respects a model of good works, and in your teaching show integrity, gravity and sound speech that cannot be censured.*
>
> Titus 2:1,6-8 (NRSV)

Paul also adds:

> *These, then, are the things you should teach.*
>
> Titus 2:15 (NIV)

Points for Reflection

What should the Christian stance be? First of all, we should accept any person unconditionally who identifies as LGBT or who has gender dysphoria, because all humans are made in the image of God and we are commanded to 'love one another'. However, the Bible is clear and unambiguous: sexual activity outside of marriage is immoral and is forbidden. Any attempts to disguise their gender and deceive others by cross-dressing or any other deviant behaviour is sinful and contrary to God's divine intentions. We are reminded it is not our place to be provocative or judgmental, but to be kind and understanding. In the case of those struggling with urges they cannot control, we are to be sympathetic as they may need professional counselling. Paul appreciates we all have struggles with sin.

> *We know that the whole creation has been groaning in labour pains until now, we ourselves groan inwardly while we wait for adoption, the redemption of our bodies.*
>
> Romans 8:22-23 (NRSV)

We are to remember that God is our judge. However, we have a responsibility to be willing to discuss and explain what the Bible teaches on the subject of sexual morality and godly behaviour. We should remember we are all sinners saved by grace and should pray for those struggling with sin.

In particular, our prayer should be they will gain insight with the help of the Holy Spirit, realize the truth, repent of their sin and accept Jesus Christ into their lives as their personal Saviour.

A Personal Challenge

Our examination of these sensitive issues should act as an incentive to accept this challenge:

> *Do not be conformed to the world, but be transformed by the renewal of your mind, that by testing you may discern what is the will of God, what is good and acceptable and perfect.*
>
> Romans 12:2 (ESV)

Questions

Why does society believe everyone should be able to live his or her life as they please?

_____

_____

Given that all LGBT persons are by definition homosexuals, is it acceptable to self-identify as LGBT, providing you remain celibate?

_____

_____

How should Christians react to LGBT persons they meet socially or at work?

_____

_____

How should you treat LGBT persons in your church?

_____

_____

How do you deal with leaders in your church who are LGBT?

_____

_____

Are there any circumstances where God would bless a gay marriage?

_____

_____

CHAPTER NINE

Should Mercy-Killing Be Made Legal?

Introduction

Euthanasia is the practice of intentionally ending a person's life to relieve pain and suffering. It is the overarching term for 'mercy killing' or 'assisted suicide' and is illegal in the UK. The Greek word *eu thanatos* means 'to have a good death' and is where the word 'euthanasia' comes from.

Euthanasia has become a serious contemporary issue in recent years and those advocating assisted suicide consider a civilized society should amend the law to allow euthanasia to take place.

A recent opinion poll conducted in the UK by Care Not Killing found 73% of persons agreed with the principle of changing the law to allow assisted suicide, although 42% of those in favour had significant reservations.

Moral and Ethical Issues

Christians have differing views on what constitutes a good death and whether or not the quality of life is more important than the sanctity of life.

The moral and religious arguments have led Christians to question whether they should ever contemplate ending their life this way. The growing availability of hospices for end of life care coupled with the development of palliative care as an effective medical specialism has made the case for assisted suicide less valid.

Doctors do become involved in making *end of life decisions* for hospital patients where treatment has to be discontinued because they are unable to treat a terminal condition. However, these difficult decisions made where treatment is proving to be ineffective are not the same as making *life-ending* decisions, which is assisted suicide.

We will examine these issues from a biblical perspective and address the 'sanctity of life' debate, as well as exploring the purpose of life. This study will also examine the evidence of how significant biblical characters ended their lives.

The Sanctity of Life

The Bible teaches that God made human beings in the image of God and that makes us unique among all the living things he created.

> *Then God said, "Let Us (Father, Son, Holy Spirit) make man in Our image, according to Our likeness (not physical, but a spiritual personality and moral likeness); and let them have complete authority ... over the entire earth."*
>
> Genesis 1:26 (AMP)

Most Christians are against euthanasia, based on the belief that life is given by God and that we are made in the image of God. This makes us special in God's eyes and our lives are very precious to him. The apostle Paul likens our bodies to the temple of the Holy Spirit, for this is where the Spirit of God resides in the lives of believers.

> *Do you not know that your body is a temple of the Holy Spirit within you, which you have from God.*
>
> 1 Corinthians 6:19 (NRSV)

> *If anyone destroys God's temple, God will destroy that person. For God's temple is holy, and you are that temple.*
>
> 1 Corinthians 3:17 (NRSV)

The Roman Catholic view is that euthanasia is a grave violation of the law of God, since it is the deliberate killing of a human being. At Mount Sinai God gave Moses the Ten Commandments, which are concise and unambiguous:

> *You shall not murder.*
>
> Exodus 20:13 (ESV)

Jesus not only supports the Old Testament law regarding the sanctity of life, but raises the standard, pointing out that if you are even angry with your brother or sister you will be judged. Anger can lead to murder. Both are sinful and Jesus makes no distinction between grave or minor sins.

Jesus said:

> "You have heard it was said to those of ancient times, 'You shall not murder' and 'whoever murders shall be liable to judgment.' But I say to you that if you are angry with a brother or sister, you will be liable to the council: and if you say, 'You fool,' you will be liable to the hell of fire."
>
> *Matthew 5:21-22 (NRSV)*

The first principle to establish is that human life is sacred. We are not to take the life of anybody else; this is a serious crime.

> *Precious in the sight of the LORD is the death of his faithful ones.*
>
> *Psalms 116:15 (NRSV)*

The Death Penalty

The penalty for murder in the Old Testament was quite clear: death.

> *Whoever takes a human life shall surely be put to death.*
>
> *Leviticus 24:17 (ESV)*

Justice would normally be carried out by the next of kin who would have the lawful right to kill the perpetrator.

> *The avenger of blood is the one who shall put the murderer to death: when they meet, the avenger of blood shall execute the sentence.*
>
> *Numbers 35:19 (NRSV)*

It is only later on that mitigating circumstances were taken into account, which allowed for a lesser penalty to be exacted for the death of a person.

Nevertheless, whilst mitigating circumstances could be taken into account in the case of manslaughter or an accidental death, there were still serious consequences for taking another person's life.

> *But if someone pushes another suddenly without enmity, or hurls any object without lying in wait, or, whilst handling any stone that could cause death, unintentionally drops it on another and death ensues, though they were not enemies and*

> *no harm was intended, then the congregation shall judge ... and rescue the slayer from the avenger of blood.*
>
> *Numbers 35:22-25 (NRSV)*

The consequences for accidentally killing someone or causing the death of somebody through thoughtless and reckless actions were compassionate, providing the death was not a premeditated act. The community would banish the perpetrator to a city of refuge, where they would be safe, providing they never strayed outside the city walls during the lifetime of the high priest, who acted as the equivalent of the judge. After the judge had died the perpetrator could return home. It was effectively a life sentence of banishment.

What Is the Purpose of Life?

In practice, we have no control over life events or the timing of such events, including when we die.

> *No one has any say-so regarding the day of death.*
>
> *Ecclesiastes 8:8 (MSG)*

These things are only known to God and are deliberately kept from us, for our own good. Imagine how anxious you would feel if you knew when and how you would die, especially as the day and time drew closer.

> *For everything there is a season, and a time for every matter under heaven, a time to be born, and a time to die.*
>
> *Ecclesiastes 3:1-2 (NRSV)*

When God allowed Job to be tempted by Satan, Job was left wondering what the purpose of life was, as ultimately he lost everything. He lost all his family, his possessions and experienced prolonged physical and mental suffering. Life became unbearable for him, but Job continued to be faithful to God and recognized he was powerless to control life events or even influence his own circumstances.

> *...Job opened his mouth and cursed the day of his birth. ... "Why did I not die at birth?"*
>
> *Job 3:1,11 (ESV)*

Although Job suffered enormously at the hands of Satan, he blessed God throughout his ordeal. He became philosophical about life once he realized God has absolute control over all things, and was able to accept God's divine will.

> Job said, "Naked I came from my mother's womb, and naked shall I return. The LORD gave, and the LORD has taken away, blessed be the name of the LORD."
>
> Job 1:21 (ESV)

Job was perplexed as to why he was suffering when he had lived a righteous life. It seemed arbitrary and unfair that suffering and prosperity are not apportioned according to the good or evil a person does. However, although he admitted he could not work out this conundrum, he knew God is wise, just and righteous compared to human beings.

> "But where, oh where, will they find Wisdom?
>   Where does Insight hide?
> Mortals don't have a clue,
>   haven't the slightest idea where to look."
>
> Job 28:12 (MSG)

The important lesson to draw from this is, Job knew when he died he would meet God as his Redeemer.

> "And he said to man,
> 'Behold the fear of the LORD, that is wisdom,
>   and to turn away from evil is understanding.'"
>
> Job 28:28 (ESV)

Euthanasia in the Bible

In the book of Judges, we learn how King Abimelech of Israel invaded the city of Thebez and whilst trying to burn down a strong tower within the city, met his fate when an upper millstone was dropped on his head. A millstone was used to grind grain and a complete millstone would weigh hundreds of pounds.

> But as he approached the entrance to the tower to set it on fire, a woman dropped an upper millstone on his head and cracked his skull. Hurriedly he called to his armor-bearer, "Draw your sword and kill me, so that they can't say, 'A

woman killed him.'" So his servant ran him through, and he died.

Judges 9:52-54 (NIV)

Clearly Abimelech was in agony and knew he was going to die and asked his armour-bearer to save his honour. He was also suffering excruciating pain from his crushed and fractured skull which he would not have survived. This is the only definite example of euthanasia in the Old Testament.

We are not told whether there were any consequences for his armour-bearer following this act of assisted suicide, but we do know it ended the rebellion and the Israelite soldiers returned home once they saw that Abimelech was dead.

A Suicide With Unintended Consequences

The following example is an account of an unsuccessful assisted suicide. The Israelites had been fighting the Philistines at the Battle of Gilboa but had suffered a serious defeat. Saul's army was wiped out and his three sons were all killed, and Saul had been very seriously wounded by the Philistines' archers. Upon realizing he was mortally wounded and likely to be tortured, abused and humiliated when captured by the enemy, Saul asked his armour-bearer to kill him.

Then Saul said to his armour-bearer, "Draw your sword and thrust me through with it, so that these uncircumcised may not come and thrust me through, and make sport of me." But his armour-bearer was unwilling, for he was terrified. So Saul took his own sword, and fell upon it. When his armour-bearer saw that Saul was dead, he also fell upon his sword, and died with him.

1 Samuel 31:4-5 (NRSV)

Next, we fast forward to an account concerning Saul's death where another soldier claims to have assisted Saul to commit suicide and we learn David's reaction to what he believed was the assisted suicide of Saul.

The twist in this whole story is that an opportunist soldier thought he could ingratiate himself with David, by telling him the news his chief enemy was dead. He hoped to receive some reward so he concocted the following story:

> *"I just happened by Mount Gilboa and came upon Saul, badly wounded and leaning on his spear, with enemy chariots and horsemen bearing down hard on him. He looked behind him, saw me, and called me to him. 'Yes sir,' I said, 'at your service.' He asked me who I was, and I told him, 'I'm an Amalekite.' 'Come here,' he said, 'and put me out of my misery. I'm nearly dead already but my life hangs on.' So I did what he asked – I killed him. I knew he wouldn't last much longer anyway. I removed his royal headband and bracelet, and have brought them to my master. Here they are."*
>
> 2 Samuel 1:8-10 (MSG)

David was extremely upset and distressed on learning of the death of Saul and his three sons as well as learning his army had been wiped out. For the rest of the day he refused to eat and was in mourning until the evening. Later that evening, when David had recovered his composure, he interviewed the young soldier.

> *Then David spoke to the young soldier who had brought the report; "Who are you anyway?" "I'm from an immigrant family – an Amalekite." "Do you mean to say," said David, "that you weren't afraid to up and kill GOD's anointed king?" Right then he ordered one of his soldiers, "Strike him dead!" The soldier struck him and he died. "You asked for it," David told him. "You sealed your death sentence when you said you killed GOD's anointed king."*
>
> 2 Samuel 1:13-16 (MSG)

This account shows David was unwilling to condone euthanasia, particularly as he knew Saul was God's anointed one. If we assume he believed the young soldier's account, David considered his actions amounted to murder and dealt with him according to the law.

> *Anyone who strikes a person with a fatal blow is to be put to death.*
>
> Exodus 21:12 (NIV)

Acts of Suicide

After the evil King Baasha died, he was succeeded by his son Elah who reigned in Tirzah for two years. His reign came to a premature end, then Zimri, a palace administrator, devised a plot to overthrow him and succeeded in killing Elah when he was drunk. Zimri appointed himself king, but he was such a disreputable person his reign only lasted seven days because the Israelites were so outraged, they attacked Tirzah in order to kill King Zimri.

> *When Zimri saw that he was surrounded and as good as dead, he entered the palace citadel, set the place on fire, and died. It was a fit end for his sins, for living a flagrantly evil life before God.*
>
> *1 Kings 16:18-19 (MSG)*

On another occasion we learn how Absalom was out to kill David, his great rival. He had a great opportunity to achieve that objective when David was cornered and in a vulnerable place. Absalom sought tactical advice from Ahithophel who advised him to take twelve thousand men and chase after David immediately. Ahithophel was upset and disillusioned when Absalom preferred the advice of Hushai. Hushai appealed to Absalom's vanity and suggested waiting until he was able to gather together his whole army and personally lead the pursuit and capture of David. However, Hushai was loyal to David and was able to warn him of Absalom's plans and the resultant delay allowed David to escape. This was a bitter blow for Ahithophel, who was a proud counsellor of both David and Absalom. His advice was always sound and his advice had never been disregarded before, but this time God intervened and arranged for Hushai's advice to appeal to Absalom more than the prudent advice of Ahithophel. When his advice was turned down, it was more than his pride could stand.

> *When Ahithophel saw that his counsel was not followed, he saddled his donkey and went off home to his own city. He set his house in order, and hanged himself. He died and was buried in the tomb of his father.*
>
> *2 Samuel 17:23 (NRSV)*

Although Ahithophel's pride was wounded, he realized that had his advice been followed, David would have faced certain death. Now that David had escaped Absalom's army, it would only be a matter of time before Absalom's army would be defeated by David. He knew David would have him killed when he learned of his disloyalty.

Difficult Questions for Christians

Suicide: An Act of Revenge

Disobeying God always has consequences, as Samson found out to his cost. Samson was brought up as a Nazarene, which meant he was not permitted to cut his hair or drink alcohol. Against the advice of his parents, Samson married a Philistine woman from Timnah, even though it was strictly forbidden for an Israelite to marry a Gentile.

The marriage broke down before the honeymoon could take place, so he visited a prostitute in Gaza, before taking a mistress named Delilah, another Philistine woman, who lived in the Valley of Sorek. She was offered eleven hundred pieces of silver by each of the five Philistines rulers,[104] which was an enormous bribe, to trick Samson into revealing the secret of his great strength.

Samson eventually succumbed to Delilah's constant nagging and told her the secret of how God had granted him great strength, providing he never cut his hair. On learning his secret, she betrayed him to the Philistines, who overpowered him, gouged out his eyes, cut his hair, shackled him in chains and put him in a prison in Gaza, where he had to work on a treadmill and became a laughing stock to the Philistines.

After his hair started to grow again, Samson was taken to a great sacrifice the Philistines were holding to worship their idol Dagon. They were celebrating Samson's capture and praising their god Dagon for delivering Samson into their hands. Samson repented to God for his sins of disobedience and asked God for a final opportunity to take revenge on the Philistines. He asked God to strengthen him one last time, knowing it would cost him his life.

> *Then Samson grasped the two middle pillars on which the house rested and he leaned his weight against them, his right hand on one and his left hand on the other. Then Samson said, "Let me die with the Philistines." He strained with all his might; and the house fell on the lords and all the people who were in it. So those killed at his death were more than those he had killed during his life.*
>
> *Judges 16:29-30 (NRSV)*

---

[104] See Judges 16:5

Death is a Consequence of Sin

The wages of sin is death.

Romans 6:23 (NIV)

Judas Iscariot, one of Jesus' disciples, will always be remembered for his betrayal of Jesus in the Garden of Gethsemane where the chief priests and elders arrested him and handed him over to Pilate the Governor for trial.

When Judas Iscariot realized the enormity of what he had done, he repented and tried to redeem the situation by confronting the chief priests and elders, but was unsuccessful.

When Judas, his betrayer, saw that Jesus was condemned, he repented and brought back the thirty pieces of silver to the chief priests and elders. He said, "I have sinned by betraying innocent blood." But they said, "What is that to us? See to it yourself." Throwing down the pieces of silver in the temple, he departed; and he went and hanged himself.

Matthew 27:3-5 (NRSV)

The question arises whether committing suicide has consequences. There is no direct condemnation of suicide in the Bible although the taking of any life is contrary to God's will. The Bible considers suicide to be self-murder, because God is the only one who can decide how and when a person will die.

Those who commit suicide are generally suffering from extreme stress, mental anguish, anxiety and depression. They feel their circumstances and prospects are completely hopeless. Suicide is undoubtedly an immense tragedy for the person concerned and a huge shock to the immediate family.

However, there is nothing in the Bible to indicate that committing suicide is an unforgiveable sin. The Bible clearly teaches that if you believe in Jesus Christ you will go to heaven.

Jesus said to her, "I am the resurrection and the life. Those who believe in me, even though they die, will live, and everyone who lives and believes in me will never die."

John 11:25-26 (NRSV)

Resisting Temptation

Life has its joys and its heartaches. Some life events can become overwhelming and tragedy can strike without warning, leaving the most resilient of people feeling helpless and unable to cope.

The apostle Paul describes these trials as satanic attacks which God allows to happen. God sends his comforter the Holy Spirit and power from on high, to enable us to resist and cope with all the trials and temptations we will face. This includes the temptation, when facing extreme distress, of contemplating committing suicide – a temptation that must always be resisted.

> *No testing has overtaken you that is not common to everyone. God is faithful, and he will not let you be tested beyond your strength, but with the testing he will also provide the way out so that you may be able to endure it.*
>
> 1 Corinthians 10:13 (NRSV)

God has a plan for each of our lives that he wants us to achieve. Life has purpose and meaning, even if sometimes we lose sight of the bigger picture.

> *For I know the plans I have for you, says the LORD, plans for your welfare and not for harm to give you a future with hope.*
>
> Jeremiah 29:11 (NRSV)

God's Promises

God has promised to provide us with the spiritual strength and power we need to cope with anything life throws at us. We are not to limit what God can do, but face the challenges of life with confidence.

> *God can do anything, you know – far more than you could ever imagine or guess or request in your wildest dreams! He does it not by pushing us around but by working within us, his Spirit deeply and gently within us.*
>
> Ephesians 3:20-21 (MSG)

God has promised to be our constant companion, to protect us throughout our lives and for all eternity. His promise is unconditional, irrespective of what persecution or extreme hardship we experience.

> *"Never will I leave you; never will I forsake you." So we say with confidence, "The Lord is my helper; I will not be afraid. What can mere mortals do to me?"*
>
> *Hebrews 13:6 (NIV)*

The day is coming when we will be forever with our heavenly Father. When that day comes, pain, suffering and distress will finally be defeated.

> *He will wipe away every tear from their eyes; and there will no longer be death; there will no longer be sorrow and anguish, or crying, or pain; for the former order of things has passed away.*
>
> *Revelation 21:4 (AMP)*

We are encouraged to remember we have a very special relationship with God. If we have accepted the good news of salvation, we become adopted into God's family and become his children.

> *Dear friends, now we are children of God, and what we will be has not yet been made known. But we know that when Christ appears, we shall be like him, for we shall see him as he is.*
>
> *1 John 3:2-3 (NIV)*

Points for Reflection

The Bible is clear that life will be a challenging experience and nobody is excused from physical and mental hardship and spiritual battles. The intensity of persecution and anguish that some have to contend with can drive them to despair where they contemplate ending their lives prematurely.

The Bible teaches that life is precious to God and taking a life is strictly forbidden, and that includes assisted suicide. Life is a gift from God. He has a plan for each one of our lives and we do not have the right to prematurely end our lives. Even when we judge the quality of our life is minimal, we are encouraged to resist the temptation to think about ending our lives.

We are fortunately able to take advantage of the huge advances in medical care that have taken place in recent decades. God has placed people with particular skills in our hospitals to help us treat a wide range of physical and mental illnesses. This generation does not have to rely exclusively on care being provided by family members and relatives when we are in the terminal stages of our lives. We have the opportunity to access palliative care, and the hospice service is a wonderful resource available to care for those who are terminally ill.

God has invited us to pray to him for healing of the mind or body. He has also placed within the wider church body Spirit-filled, anointed people with a healing ministry, which is a gift from God.

James advises any who are sick to call for the elders of the church to anoint them with oil and pray for healing.

> *Are there any among you suffering? They should pray. ... Are any among you sick? They should call for the elders of the church and have them pray over them, anointing them with oil in the name of the Lord. The prayer of faith will save the sick, and the Lord will raise them up, and anyone who has committed sins will be forgiven. Therefore confess your sins to one another, and pray for one another, so that you may be healed. The prayer of a righteous man is powerful and effective.*
>
> James 5:13a, 14-16 (NRSV)

A Personal Challenge

Psalm 23 reminds us that God is the Good Shepherd. He is our Provider, our Comforter and Protector. His love is unwavering and everlasting.

> *Surely your goodness and love will follow me all the days of my life, and I will dwell in the house of the LORD forever.*
>
> Psalm 23:6 (NIV)

Need Help?

Anyone suffering physical or mental distress which has become so overwhelming that they have become depressed and have considered ending their lives should seek professional help urgently. God views your life as very precious and it is not his will that you die by your own hand. Please seek help from your G.P., counsellor, minister or the Samaritans[105].

---

[105] *www.samaritans.org;* freephone 116-123

Questions

How is a Christian to cope with an incurable, degenerate disease?

_____
_____

How do you respond to a dying family member who wants to go to a clinic for euthanasia?

_____
_____

Are there any circumstances where it would be understandable for a Christian to commit suicide?

_____
_____

Are there any circumstances where it would be acceptable for a Christian to assist another to commit suicide?

_____
_____

Does it matter whether a Christian is buried or cremated?

_____
_____

Is it appropriate for a Christian to make a living will?

_____
_____

CHAPTER TEN

Are Angels Real?

Introduction

Do you believe in angels? What do you think when someone mentions angels to you? Does the Robbie Williams song *Angels* spring to mind or do you recall the carol *Angels from the Realms of Glory*?

For most of us, the significance of angels in the Bible is not something we think about except at Christmastime.

Although some people do not think angels are very significant, the Bible has a great deal to say about them, and they are mentioned two hundred and seventy-three times. This is apart from references to Satan, the fallen angel, and his followers, who are mentioned thirty-five times in the New Testament.

On examining what the Bible says about angels, we need to identify their characteristics, their roles and the powers delegated to them. We will look at angels in the life of Jesus, what he says about them and what impact they had on those who saw them.

Angels and Archangels

The Greek word for angel is *angelos*. Angels are spiritual beings and one of their roles is to appear to humans and communicate important messages from God. Angels are only referred to in the Bible in the masculine gender. For example, when the Lord appeared to Abraham in the form of three angels, they were all dressed in men's clothing.[106]

Some of the angels have specific roles to perform and are known by their name. The angel Gabriel is mentioned nine times in the Bible, and

---

[106] See Genesis 18:2

he is one of God's chief messengers. He made important announcements from God, such as when he appeared to the virgin Mary.

> *God sent the angel Gabriel ... to a virgin pledged to be married to a man named Joseph.*
>
> *Luke 1:26 (NIV)*

On one occasion Daniel receives an 'end time' vision from the angel Gabriel about a future fierce conflict he is involved in against the demonic Prince of Persia, which involved twenty-one days of intense fighting.

> *But I (Gabriel) will tell you what is inscribed in the writing of truth. There is no one who stands firmly with me and strengthens himself against these (hostile forces) except Michael, your prince (the guardian of your nation).*
>
> *Daniel 10:21 (AMP)*

The Greek word *archangelos* means a 'chief angel'. According to Jewish tradition there are seven archangels, but the archangel Michael is the only one mentioned in the Bible by name. The archangel Michael, it is prophesied, will make himself known in the 'end times' when the world is judged. He is known as 'the great prince who protects your people'[107]. The archangel Michael is mentioned fifteen times in the Bible and is one of God's chief advocates and trouble-shooters.

> *Even the archangel Michael, when he was disputing with the devil about the body of Moses, did not himself dare to condemn him for slander but said, "The Lord rebuke you!"*
>
> *Jude 1:9 (NIV)*

Cherubim and *Seraphim*

Cherubim are winged heavenly beings known as 'throne angels' because they are found in the vicinity of God's throne. Isaiah describes their role as guarding the throne in heaven.

> *LORD Almighty, the God of Israel, enthroned between the cherubim, you alone are God over all the kingdoms of the earth. You have made heaven and earth.*
>
> *Isaiah 37:16 (NIV)*

---

[107] Daniel 12:1 (NIV)

When Adam and Eve sinned and were driven out of the Garden of Eden, God made sure there was no possibility they could return.

> *After he drove the man out, he placed on the east side of the Garden of Eden cherubim and a flaming sword flashing back and forth to guard the way to the tree of life.*
>
> Genesis 3:24 (NIV)

Seraphim burn with a passion to worship God. They fly above God's throne in heaven and are the closest angels to God. The word *seraphim* comes from the Hebrew word for 'passion' which means 'to burn'. Their primary role is to conduct praise and worship to God and celebrate his holiness and perfect love.

> *I saw the Lord, high and exalted, seated on a throne; and the train of his robe filled the temple. Above him were seraphim, each with six wings: With two wings they covered their faces, with two they covered their feet, and with two they were flying. And they were calling to one another:*
> *"Holy, holy, holy is the LORD Almighty;*
> *the whole earth is full of his glory."*
>
> Isaiah 6:1-3 (NIV)

Satan, the Fallen Angel

Whilst angels are created by God and operate under the authority of God, they are able to exercise free will. Their primary role of is to worship and serve God, and Satan was originally a very special *cherub* before his expulsion from heaven.

> *You were the anointed cherub who covers and protects, and I placed you there. You were on the holy mountain of God ... You were blameless in your ways from the day you were created until unrighteousness and evil were found in you.*
>
> Ezekiel 28:14-15 (AMP)

Satan was a beautiful, but proud and rebellious cherub who was expelled from heaven by God because he challenged him and wanted to take over ruling the universe. After Jesus had appointed seventy evangelists to preach the gospel ahead of him, he told them he had witnessed Satan's spectacular demise.

> *"I watched Satan fall from heaven like (a flash of) lightning."*
>
> Luke 10:18 (AMP)

> *Your heart was proud and arrogant because of your beauty. You destroyed your wisdom for the sake of your splendour. I cast you to the ground...*
>
> Ezekiel 28:17 (AMP)

Satan was in charge of a large contingent of angels who became known as 'fallen angels'. These rebellious angels, which comprised a third of all the angels in heaven, were ejected from heaven along with Satan.

Prior to his expulsion from heaven, the cherub Satan was a very talented musician whom God had appointed, according to many theologians, to be the worship leader of all the heavenly angels in heaven.

> *The workmanship of your timbrels and pipes was prepared for you on the day you were created.*
>
> Ezekiel 28:13 (NKJV)

The timbrel, or *tabret*, was the principal percussion instrument of the Israelites.

> *Your pomp and magnificence have been brought down to Sheol, along with the music of your harps.*
>
> Isaiah 14:11 (AMP)

When the word *Sheol* was translated from the Hebrew into the Greek, the word *Hades* was used instead to make it clear that Satan is evil.

Satan is referred to in the Bible by a number of names. These include 'the Devil'[108], 'Lucifer', the 'ancient serpent'[109], the 'Evil One'[110], the 'Great Dragon'[111], the 'prince of demons'[112] and the 'roaring lion'[113].

He also masquerades as an 'angel of light'[114], with the aim of deceiving humans. These fallen angels, under the leadership of Satan, spend their time tempting, taunting, deceiving, afflicting, stirring up people and working to alienate people from God.

---

[108] Matthew 12:24 (NIV)
[109] Revelation 12:9 (ESV)
[110] 1 John 5:18 (ESV)
[111] Revelation 12:9 (ESV)
[112] Matthew 12:24 (NIV)
[113] 1 Peter 5:8 (NIV)
[114] 2 Corinthians 11:14 (AMP)

Characteristics of Angels

Angels were created by God to live eternally. They were created at the same time as heaven and earth were formed and they were in existence even before humans were created.

The word 'created' comes from the Hebrew word *bara*, which means 'to make something out of nothing'; as opposed to the word 'make' which means 'to assemble or construct from something else'.

Angels are spiritual beings and although they do not have physical bodies, they are able to appear on occasions in human form. They do not marry or produce offspring.

> *"At the resurrection people will neither marry nor be given in marriage; they will be like angels in heaven."*
>
> Matthew 22:30 (NIV)

When believers go to heaven to be with God, they will be spirit beings like angels. Jesus told the Sadducees, who claim there is no resurrection, that those who believe in the resurrection from the dead will live forever with God as part of his family.

> *"But those who are considered worthy of taking part in the age to come and in the resurrection from the dead will neither marry nor be given in marriage, and they can no longer die; for they are like the angels."*
>
> Luke 20:35-36 (NIV)

Although all references to angels in the Bible are as men, that is not the same as being genderless; all the following references to angels are as men: Genesis 18:2; Ezekiel 9:3; Zechariah 1:19; Revelation 10:1; Revelation 14:18 and Revelation 20:1.

At least some angels have wings and the ability to fly.

> *I saw another angel flying in mid-air, and he had the eternal gospel to proclaim to those who live on the earth.*
>
> Revelation 14:6 (NIV)

Sometimes their appearance is dazzling in bright, shiny clothing; other times they imitate human beings and appear inconspicuously.

An angel appeared with six armed men to Ezekiel the prophet. With them was a man clothed in linen with a 'writing kit at his side'[115].

A spectacular appearance can be seen in the book of Daniel, after he had completed a period of fasting and was standing on the bank of the River Tigris accompanied by his servants. The effect on Daniel was traumatic and overwhelming. He was left completely helpless, drained of any strength, hardly able to breathe, and he turned a deathly pale shade. He fell trembling to his hands and knees and was speechless. However, that was nothing compared to his servants who were so terrified, they ran away and went into hiding.

> *I looked up and there before me was a man dressed in linen with a belt of fine gold from Uphaz around his waist. His body like topaz, his face like lightning, his eyes like flaming torches, his arms and legs like the gleam of burnished bronze, and his voice like the sound of a multitude.*
>
> Daniel 10:5-6 (NIV)

Following the crucifixion of Jesus, he was buried in a new tomb belonging to Joseph of Arimathea and the tomb was sealed with a great stone. At daybreak on the Sabbath, Mary and Mary Magdalene went to see the tomb.

> *And suddenly there was a great earthquake; for an angel of the Lord, descending from heaven, came and rolled back the stone and sat on it. His appearance was like lightning, and his clothing white as snow. For fear of him the guards shook and became like dead men.*
>
> Matthew 28:2-4 (NRSV)

Angels are wise, intelligent spiritual beings, who are able to discern good from evil. They are able to pass on wisdom, knowledge and understanding, as Daniel discovered when the angel Gabriel appeared to him in a vision.

> *"Daniel, I have now come to give you insight and understanding. As soon as you began to pray, a word went*

---

[115] Ezekiel 9:3 (NIV)

out, which I have come to tell you, for you are highly esteemed."

Daniel 9:22-23 (NIV)

Angels are emotional spiritual beings capable of expressing their feelings and rejoicing when someone who is not a follower of Jesus becomes born again and becomes part of his heavenly family.

> "I say to you there is joy in the presence of the angels of God over one sinner who repents."

Luke 15:10 (NKJV)

Living with Angels

All believers who have accepted Jesus Christ as their personal Saviour and whose names are written in the 'Lamb's Book of Life'[116] will live happily with the angels in heaven for all eternity.

> You have come to thousands and thousands of angels in joyful assembly, to the church of the firstborn, whose names are written in heaven.

Hebrews 12:22 (NIV)

In the Apostle John's vision, he recalls seeing so many in Heaven he was unable to count them, but estimated there were ten thousand times ten thousand which is one hundred million – but even this figure may be an underestimate.

> Then I looked and heard the voice of many angels, numbering thousands upon thousands, and ten thousands times ten thousands.

Revelation 5:11 (NIV)

We learn Jesus is all-powerful and has tremendous authority, as he reigns alongside God in heaven.

> Jesus has the last word on everything and everyone from angels to armies. He's standing right alongside God and what he says goes.

1 Peter 3:22 (MSG)

---

[116] Revelation 21:27 (AMP)

Nobody else is worthy of our worship except God. When we pray, we have direct access to God through his son Jesus Christ.

> *The Spirit Himself testifies and confirms together with our spirit (assuring us) that we (believers) are children of God. And if (we are His) children (then we are His) heirs also: heirs of God and fellow heirs with Christ (sharing His spiritual blessing and inheritance), if indeed we share in His suffering so that we may also share in His glory.*
>
> Romans 8:16-17 (AMP)

The Bible teaches that believers will be the judges of angels and we will sit alongside Jesus on his throne.

> *Do you not know we are to judge angels?*
>
> 1 Corinthians 6:3 (ESV)

This is why we are warned not to worship or pray to them, because their status in heaven is not the same as ours. The angels know their role and their place in the order of things, as the apostle John discovered when he was given an insight into heaven and the glorious majesty of God by an angel of the Lord in his 'end time' vision. He was overwhelmed by what he was witnessing.

> *"These are the true words of God." Then I fell down at his feet to worship him, but he said to me, "You must not do that! I am a fellow servant with you and your brothers who hold to the testimony of Jesus. Worship God." For the testimony of Jesus is the spirit of prophecy.*
>
> Revelation 19:10 (ESV)

Angels as Messengers from God

One of the main roles of angels was to act as messengers from God.

> *Now an angel of the Lord said to Philip, "Go south to the road – the desert road – that goes down from Jerusalem to Gaza."*
>
> Acts 8:26 (NIV)

Luke describes how Phillip was told by an angel to go to Gaza to meet an Ethiopian eunuch in his chariot and explain to him the meaning of what he was reading in the book of Isaiah.

> *Then Philip began with that very passage of Scripture and told him the good news about Jesus.*
>
> Acts 8:35 (NIV)

The outcome was that he was baptized and became a follower of Jesus Christ.

An angel appeared to Cornelius, the Roman Centurion, in a vision.

> *He distinctly saw an angel of God, who came to him and said, "Cornelius!"*
>
> Acts 10:3 (NIV)

Cornelius was a devout man so he sent for Simon Peter for an interpretation of the vision. Fortunately, Peter also received a vision and was able to explain to Cornelius how God had revealed to him that the message of salvation was not just for the Jews but for everybody in the world.

King Herod began to persecute Christians in earnest and had Peter arrested, bound with chains and thrown into prison with a guard of sixteen soldiers. The night before his trial was scheduled to take place an angel appeared.

> *Suddenly an angel of the Lord appeared and a light shone in the cell.*
>
> Acts 12:7 (NIV)

Peter was woken up by the angel, released from his chains and told to get dressed. He was then escorted past the guards and out of the prison. Herod was so annoyed he had escaped and couldn't be found, that he had the guards responsible executed.

Luke records another incident when Paul was being transported as a prisoner to Rome. The sea journey was very dangerous and they took such a battering from the stormy seas, they were forced to dump the cargo overboard in order to give themselves a chance of saving their boat from sinking. On the fourteenth night, near the island of Clauda, an angel appeared to Paul.

> *"Last night an angel of the God to whom I belong and whom I serve stood beside me and said, 'Do not be afraid, Paul. You must stand trial before Caesar; and God has graciously given you the lives of all who sail with you.'"*
>
> Acts 27:23-24 (NIV)

They continued until the boat hit a sandbar and went aground, broke up and was destroyed in the ensuing shipwreck. On board were two hundred and seventy-six people; all of them made it safely to shore, as promised by the angel of the Lord.

In this final passage, Jesus reveals God's plan concerning end time events.

> *He made it known by sending his angel to his servant John, who testifies to everything he saw – that is, the word of God and the testimony of Jesus Christ.*
>
> Revelation 1:1-2 (NIV)

This revelation occurred while the apostle John was on the Mediterranean island of Patmos and constitutes the book of Revelation.

Awesome Angelic Powers

While the primary purpose of angels is to worship and serve God, we should not forget they are awesome spiritual beings. God sends angels to bring good news, comfort and strength. However, they are also sent to bring judgment and punishment to those who sin against God, usually the enemies of God's people, although the Israelites were not exempt when they sinned and were disobedient.

> *It was by faith that Moses commanded the people of Israel to keep the Passover and to sprinkle blood at the doorposts so that the 'angel of death' would not kill their first-born sons.*
>
> Hebrews 11:28 (NLT)

King David became proud and arrogant and succumbed to temptation by Satan to count all his armed forces in Israel.[117] He dismissed Joab's warning and insisted the census went ahead. The outcome of the census was that he had one million, one hundred thousand soldiers in his army in Israel and a further four hundred and seventy thousand soldiers in Judah – an enormous army of one million five hundred and seventy thousand troops.

There was a terrible price to pay for his vanity and disobedience. God was very displeased and sent an angel to punish Israel with a plague, which had terrible consequences.

---

[117] See 1 Chronicles 21:1

Difficult Questions for Christians

> *So the LORD sent a pestilence on Israel; and seventy thousand persons fell in Israel. And God sent an angel to Jerusalem to destroy it; but when he was about to destroy it the LORD took note and relented concerning the calamity; he said to the destroying angel, "Enough! Stay your hand."*
>
> 1 Chronicles 21:14-15 (NRSV)

On another occasion, God used an angel to punish the Assyrians who were about to invade Jerusalem. After King Hezekiah prayed to God for deliverance from the Assyrian armies, God spoke to Hezekiah through the prophet Isaiah and promised him that King Sennacherib of Assyria would not conquer the city of Jerusalem because the Lord would defend the city.

> *That night the angel of the LORD went out and put to death a hundred and eighty-five thousand in the Assyrian camp. When the people got up the next morning – there were all the dead bodies!*
>
> 2 Kings 19:35 (NIV)

This final demonstration of angelic powers is unusual. Not only did the angel of the Lord open the cell doors and lead Peter and the apostles unseen out of the prison, but the angel shut and locked the prison doors behind them. When their disappearance was investigated, they were unable to find any evidence of their escape because the prison was still securely locked and on opening the cell doors they found nobody inside.

> *During the night an angel of the Lord opened the doors of the jail and brought them out.*
>
> Acts 5:19 (NIV)

Angels in the Life of Jesus

There were several occasions when angels appeared at critical points in the nativity story. Angels appeared to Mary and Joseph on separate occasions prior to his birth. Once Jesus was born, angels appeared to the shepherds and later on to the wise men, following which Joseph was warned about Herod's plan to kill Jesus. Finally, they returned to tell Joseph that Herod was dead and it was safe to return to Nazareth.

Apart from this intense activity around Jesus' birth, there are only two recorded instances when angels appeared to Jesus during his lifetime.

Are Angels Real?

These appearances were at critical points in his life when angels came to strengthen and support him.

The first time was when Jesus was taken to the wilderness to be tempted by Satan. During the forty days he fasted in the wilderness, the angels protected him from the wild animals.[118] Jesus was tempted in three locations by the devil; initially in the wilderness, then he was taken to the highest point of the temple in Jerusalem and finally to the top of a very high mountain. Each time Jesus resisted the temptations and finally he firmly dismissed Satan.

> *"Go away Satan! For it is written and forever remains written, 'You shall worship the Lord your God and serve him only.' Then the Devil left him; and suddenly angels came and ministered to Him bringing him food and serving Him."*
>
> Matthew 4:10-11 (AMP)

The second occasion occurred after Jesus had eaten the Passover meal with his disciples. He went up to the Mount of Olives alone to pray and asked God whether there was any other way to pay the price for the sins of the world, other than by being crucified.

> *Then an angel from heaven appeared to him and gave him strength. In his anguish he prayed more earnestly and his sweat became like great drops of blood falling down on the ground.*
>
> Luke 22:43-44 (NRSV)

Luke, ever the doctor, reports that Jesus was suffering from symptoms associated with a condition known as *hematohidrosis*, a rare condition that can be caused by extreme emotional and mental stress. Luke explains the extreme pressure Jesus was under, faced with the prospect of being humiliated, tortured and cruelly crucified at Calvary.

Jesus makes an interesting reference to the power of angels at his betrayal in the Garden of Gethsemane. When Judas Iscariot came to betray him, accompanied by the chief priests and elders and a large crowd armed with swords and clubs, Peter acted to defend Jesus. He drew his sword and struck Malchus, one of the high priest's servants, cutting off his right ear, but Jesus told him to put his sword away.

---

[118] See Mark 1:13

> "Do you think I cannot call on my Father, and he will at once put at my disposal more than twelve legions of angels? But how then would the Scriptures be fulfilled that say it must happen in this way?"
>
> Matthew 26:53-54 (NIV)

Twelve legions of angels is about seventy-two thousand angels and Jesus said he could call down more than that number. A single angel has the strength to kill one hundred and eighty-five thousand Assyrians.[119]

On that basis twelve legions of angels would have been able to kill over one billion people!

This demonstrates the awesome power and authority Jesus had at his command, but he was determined to be obedient to God and carry out his plan to save humanity from the consequences of their sin.

Jesus appeared to his disciples for forty days after his resurrection until the time came for his ascension to heaven. When this occurred, witnessed by his disciples, two angels appeared and prophesied his future return and offered reassurance and comfort.

> While he was going and they were gazing up towards heaven, suddenly two men in white robes stood by them. "This Jesus, who has been taken up from you into heaven, will come in the same way as you saw him go into heaven."
>
> Acts 1:10-11 (NRSV)

What the Bible Says About Spiritual Conflict

The Bible warns us that because of our sinful nature there is serious tension between the forces of good and evil. The Apostle Paul sums it up succinctly, admitting that he is full of good intentions and tries to do good, but is unable to carry it out.

> For if I know the law but still can't keep it, and if the power of sin within me keeps sabotaging my best intentions, I obviously need help! I realize that I don't have what it takes. I can will it, but I can't do it.
>
> Romans 7:17-18 (MSG)

---

[119] See Isaiah 37:36

Are Angels Real?

It is important that as Christians we recognize this is a spiritual conflict which we cannot win in our own strength. We must prepare for battle by putting on the full armour of God which he has provided for our protection.

> *Be prepared. You're up against far more than you can handle on your own. Take all the help you can get, every weapon God has issued, so that when it's all over but the shouting you'll still be on your feet.*
>
> *Ephesians 6:13-14 (MSG)*

Paul is clear in his letter to the Christians in the church at Ephesus that the armour we have at our disposal will enable us to defeat our enemies.

> *Stand firm and hold your ground, HAVING TIGHTENED THE WIDE BAND OF TRUTH (personal integrity and moral courage) AROUND YOUR WAIST and HAVING PUT ON THE BREASTPLATE OF RIGHTEOUSNESS (an upright heart), and having strapped on YOUR FEET THE GOSPEL OF PEACE IN PREPARATION (to face the enemy with firm-footed stability and the readiness produced by the good news). Above all, lift up the (protective) shield of faith with which you can extinguish all the flaming arrows of the evil one. And take THE HELMET OF SALVATION, and the sword of the Spirit, which is the Word of God. With all prayer and petition pray (with specific requests) at all times (on every occasion and in every season) in the Spirit, and with this in view, stay alert with all perseverance and petition (interceding in prayer) for all God's people.*
>
> *Ephesians 6:14-18 (AMP)*

The Holy Spirit lives in all Christians who believe Jesus Christ is the Son of God who died on the cross to pay the price for their sins. Those who accept him as their personal Saviour have the assurance of salvation and know he is now seated in heaven on the right side of God. The Bible reminds us of who he is, who we are and what is truth. The Holy Spirit reminds us of God's promises, which is why Paul encourages us to study God's word, meditate on it and pray, as this will change our attitudes and thought processes.

> *Do not be conformed to this world, but be transformed by the renewing of your minds, so that you may discern what is the will of God – what is good and acceptable and perfect.*
>
> Romans 12:2 (NRSV)

James, in his letter to Jewish believers scattered throughout the Roman Empire, points out that we all face challenges and difficulties in life. The testing of our faith produces perseverance and character which turns us into mature Christians. We are urged to persevere because the Lord has promised 'that person will receive the crown of life that the Lord has promised to those who love him'[120].

God predicts we will be victorious, and he makes this promise to each one of us:

> *Submit yourselves therefore to God. Resist the devil, and he will flee from you.*
>
> James 4:7 (NRSV)

Points for Reflection

It is evident that angels are both relevant today and still active in serving God and working to carry out God's plans for believers.

- Angels help people. (Daniel 6:22)
- Angels issue instructions to people. (Genesis 16:9)
- Angels deliver messages from the Lord. (Luke 1:35)
- Angels appear in visions and dreams. (Daniel 10:14)
- Angels protect people. (Exodus 23:20)
- Angels keep guard over us. (Psalm 91:11)

Angels reveal themselves as spiritual beings in spectacular and dramatic ways when they appear in all their glory and radiance, but other times they appear quietly and discretely. Although they are invisible and unseen by us, they constantly watch over and protect us.

---

[120] James 1:12 (NIV)

Are Angels Real?

> *For he will command his angels concerning you*
> *to guard you in all your ways...*
>
> Psalm 91:11 (NIV)

We know there are many millions of angels in heaven that we will meet either when we die and go to heaven, or on the day of the second coming of Jesus Christ.

> *For the Son of Man is going to come in the glory and majesty of His Father with His angels, and they will repay each one in accordance with what he has done.*
>
> Matthew 16:27 (AMP)

It follows that angels are still active, guiding, strengthening, supporting and protecting believers every day, everywhere. Paul reminds us to be vigilant and responsive to those we meet.

> *Let brotherly love continue. Do not forget to entertain strangers, for by so doing some have unwittingly entertained angels.*
>
> Hebrews 13:1-2 (NKJV)

We are warned to be prepared. We may encounter angels in our daily lives and should act appropriately as they may appear in ways we do not expect. Some Christians claim to have had modern day encounters with angels. However, the Bible also points out that Satan and his angels disguise themselves as 'angels of light' in order to deceive and lead astray anyone who will listen to them.

> *Satan himself masquerades as an angel of light. It is not surprising then if his servants also masquerade as servants of righteousness. Their end will be what their actions deserve.*
>
> 2 Corinthians 11:14-15 (NIV)

A Personal Challenge

The Bible acknowledges that we will encounter troubles and sorrows in this life that will not come to an end until Satan has been finally defeated and banished to hell for all eternity. Be encouraged, there are guardian angels watching over everyone who have accepted the free gift of salvation.

Jesus made an important promise to all believers which is recorded in this letter to the Christians in Rome:

For He Himself has said, "I will never leave you nor forsake you." So we may boldly say: "The Lord is my helper; I will not fear. What can man do to me?"

Hebrews 13:5-6 (NKJV)

Are Angels Real?

Questions

Do angels appear to people nowadays?

_____

_____

Do Christian have guardian angels assigned to protect and guide them?

_____

_____

Will Christians look like, and have the same qualities as, angels in heaven?

_____

_____

How do we discern false angels?

_____

_____

How can Christians overcome the temptations we encounter from Satan?

_____

_____

Why, if Satan is a defeated foe, do we succumb to his sinful ways?

_____

_____

Difficult Questions for Christians

CHAPTER ELEVEN

Why do Christians Celebrate Pagan Festivals?

Introduction

Christmas is the most lucrative commercial opportunity for retailers in the year and one of the most significant religious celebrations. The average family will spend nearly £900 on presents, food, drink and decorations and borrow £450 on credit cards. The total spend in the UK is over £50 billion, of which £4.2 billion is spent on food and drink. Lost production is considerable, as many people take extended holidays over the Christmas / New Year period, given the close proximity of several public holidays. Over £2.4 billion is wasted on uneaten food, discarded food and unwanted gifts; 30% more rubbish is produced than normal and our carbon footprint amounts to 5.5% of the annual total for the UK.

The Christmas holiday for some is not all unbridled happiness as the realization that excessive spending has created financial problems and debt. Extended time spent with families and relatives leads to arguments and conflict resulting in a busy time for solicitors on the first Monday after Christmas, known as 'Blue Monday', as unhappy couples commence divorce proceedings.

There is some respite for shopaholics thanks to the Christmas Day (Trading) Act 2004, as large retailers are prohibited from opening on Christmas Day, although the Internet has undermined the purpose of the Act to keep Christmas special. The idea of a minimalist Christmas appeals to some people, where the focus is on people and not things and there is no gift-giving. The idea is to spend time quietly at home enjoying each other's company. Alternatively, helping others in need by offering hospitality to those all alone, or acting as a volunteer with a local charity helping the homeless, or visiting the sick in hospital or residential care homes, are great ways for Christians to demonstrate the true spirit of Christmas.

Church attendance is popular over Christmas as over two million attend church services and a further 2.7 million support carol services.

This study of Christmas identifies the pagan origins of many of our Christmas customs and identifies shortcomings in our portrayal of the nativity story, together with other historical misconceptions about Christmas.

Another central theme concerns prophecies relating to the coming Messiah in the Old Testament and their subsequent fulfilment in the New Testament hundreds of years later. Finally, there follows a sequential account of all the pertinent events in the New Testament accounts of the birth of Jesus.

The Historical Significance of Christmas

Christmas is composed of two words. 'Christ' comes from the Greek word *Khristos* (a translation of the Hebrew word *Masiah*, which means 'Messiah'). 'Mas' is short for 'mass' and comes from the Latin word *missa*. The term Christmas comes from Christ-mass – the church service that celebrates the birth of Christ on 25th December.

Xmas originates from the early days of the Christian church when the X was used as a secret symbol to represent Christ. The X also resembles the cross, which is the symbol for Christ. *Chi* or *X* is the first letter of the Greek word for Christ.

In the early days of Christianity, the birth of Christ was not celebrated. The Bible does not mention the date for his birth and there is no requirement to celebrate his birth in the New Testament.

Originally the 25th December celebrated 'Saturnalia' in honour of the planet Saturn, the god of agriculture. An ancient historian, Livy, informs us that the Festival of Saturnalia began in 497 B.C. The Romans also celebrated the god of Mithra on 25th December, who was a god of light and friendship. It was several centuries later before church leaders decided to initiate their own day to celebrate the incarnation of God and the birth of Jesus Christ. Pope Julius 1st chose 25th December to replace the traditions of the pagan solstice festival of excessive consumption and replaced it with a joyful festival of celebration and worship to our Lord and King.

In David Pawson's book *Unlocking the Bible Omnibus*, he explains that the book of Deuteronomy warns of the dangers of syncretism, which is incorporating pagan practices into our lives, and how easily we can do it without realizing it. He points out that Christmas and Halloween were both pagan festivals which the church tried to make 'Christian' when they should have been avoided altogether.

An article by Hani Abu Dayyeh titled *Shepherding in the Land* explains the lambing season in Israel would commence during September. This was when the shepherds would have been watching their flocks overnight to protect their sheep from marauding wolves and hyenas and also to separate the female sheep from the rest of the flock after mating had taken place. He concludes that the shepherds would have visited Jesus in the stable in Bethlehem about this time. David Pawson agrees the birth of Jesus would have occurred between late September and early October and probably coincided with the week-long Jewish holiday of *Sukkot*, known as The Feast of Tabernacles, which commenced on the 15th day of Tishrei in the Jewish calendar. David Pawson believes Luke indirectly points us to the month of Jesus' birth because we learn from the first book of Chronicles that Zechariah was from the priestly tribe of Ahijah who served in the temple on an established rota basis. From the account of Elizabeth's pregnancy in Luke, it is possible to calculate when Mary gave birth to Jesus in Bethlehem.

Christmas Customs

Some of the customs that have grown up around Christmas have varying degrees of religious significance, but Christmas trees are a relatively recent tradition which only caught on in the UK when Queen Victoria introduced a tree to Windsor Castle in 1848. The practice of decorating trees with light and baubles became commonplace in the twentieth century.

Exchanging presents at Christmastime is a reminder of the gifts that were given to Jesus by the wise men. 'Gold' is associated with kings, and Christians celebrate Jesus Christ who is the King of Kings. 'Frankincense' was a perfume used in Jewish worship and represents glorifying Jesus Christ. 'Myrrh' was another perfume, but used on dead bodies to make them smell more pleasant; and reminds us Jesus Christ would have to suffer and die for our sins.

Why do Christians Celebrate Pagan Festivals?

The custom of sending Christmas cards began in 1843 by Sir Henry Cole, who helped set up the Post Office and wanted to boost custom by encouraging people to exchange Christmas greetings. The first cards produced were of the nativity scene and were designed by John Horsley.

Christmas crackers were first made around 1845-1850 by Tom Smith, a London sweet-maker, as a fun idea to boost trade, by incorporating a wrapper around sweets that, when pulled in half, made a cracking sound.

Christmas carols were originally pagan songs sung at the winter solstice. Early Christians replaced the pagan practice and composed Christian songs to sing instead.

The origins of Pantomimes can be traced back to the ancient Saturnalia mid-winter feast. For five days slaves were not required to work and in some households they would exchange roles with their masters. This role reversal led to the practice of men dressing up as women and vice versa. Pantomimes first came to the UK in the eighteenth century, although Francis of Assisi introduced nativity plays to Italy as early as 1223.

The custom of decorating homes with holly and ivy has religious significance as the holly represents the crown of thorns worn by Jesus Christ when he was crucified and the berries represent the drops of blood shed for the sins of the world. Ivy needs to cling to something to support it while it grows and this acts as a reminder to us to place our trust in God and cling to him for support in our lives.

On the other hand, Mistletoe, a hemiparasitic plant that lives off the nutrients and water of a host tree, is a symbol of romance. It was so-named by the Anglo-Saxons when they noticed how mistletoe often grows where birds leave droppings. 'Mistel' means 'dung', and 'tan' means 'twig'; hence the term 'dung-on-a-twig'. The tradition of kissing beneath the mistletoe started in ancient Greece during the pagan festival of Saturnalia and the plant is associated with fertility. It is also associated with other pagan gods like Frigga, the goddess of love.

Finally, mince pies were originally filled with meat, as were Christmas puddings, and were made in an oval shape to represent the manger at Bethlehem. Nowadays they are filled with dried fruit and spices.

There has been a return to the secular emphasis on Christmas with excessive eating and drinking, the modern equivalent of the revelry and drunkenness that was a feature of pagan festivals. In 1645 this upset the puritans so much it prompted Oliver Cromwell to ban Christmas altogether, although it was restored soon after by Charles II when he became king from 1600 until 1645, a period in history known as the Restoration.

The Biblical Accounts

All the synoptic Gospels cover the ministry, death and resurrection of Jesus, with each providing a different perspective, but only Matthew and Luke cover the birth of Jesus Christ. Matthew's account starts with the genealogy of Jesus, as he is writing to the Jews and seeks to demonstrate the lineage through the generations from David to Abraham. Abraham was the founder of Judaism and it was Moses who later received the Torah, the law of God which are the first five books of the Bible known as the Pentateuch.

Matthew highlights the prophecies recorded in the Old Testament hundreds of years previously, in order to demonstrate how the birth of Jesus fulfilled prophecies that he was the promised Messiah. Although Matthew's account includes the visit by the wise men and the murderous acts of king Herod, he omits to mention the visit by the shepherds.

Luke writes primarily for a Gentile audience and focuses on those marginalized groups like women, children, the sick and the poor, as well as neglected groups like the Samaritans. Luke's birth narrative is the most comprehensive and includes the appearances of angels to Mary and Elizabeth, but not to Joseph. He draws attention to the homeless state of Mary and Joseph in Bethlehem and their use of the feeding trough as a crib. Luke's account includes the appearance of the angels to the shepherds, who become the first messengers and witnesses to Jesus' birth, but he omits the later visit by the wise men.

Fulfilled Prophecies

Some scholars believe there are over three hundred prophecies about Jesus Christ concerning his birth, life, death and resurrection in the Old Testament.

The following four prophetic examples about the birth of Jesus are very specific and concern firstly, the virgin birth; secondly, that this would take place in Bethlehem; thirdly, that Jesus Christ would be a prophet like Moses; and finally, that he would be the promised Messiah, the Son of God.

This first prophecy was that the Messiah would be born of a virgin and would be called Immanuel. This was recorded by the prophet Isaiah in approximately 735 B.C. At this time King Ahaz was king of Judah and is portrayed as an evil king who reigned from the age of twenty for sixteen years.

Therefore the Lord himself will give you a sign: the virgin will conceive and give birth to a son, and will call him Immanuel.

Isaiah 7:14 (NIV)

Matthew records the fulfilment of this prophecy in the following way.

An angel of the Lord appeared to him in a dream and said, "Joseph son of David, do not be afraid to take Mary home as your wife, because what is conceived in her is from the Holy Spirit. She will give birth to a son, and you are to give him the name Jesus, because he will save his people from their sins." All this took place to fulfill what the Lord had said through the prophet: The virgin will conceive and give birth to a son, and they will call him Immanuel, which means "God with us."

Matthew 1:20-23 (NIV)

The second prophecy was made by the prophet Micah who recorded in around 750 B.C. that Jesus Christ would be born in Bethlehem. Micah was a contemporary of Isaiah and lived in Shephelah, a poor region. This contrasted with Isaiah who was a cousin of the king and was born in the palace. Micah prophesied throughout the reigns of King Ahaz and King Jotham; the latter was a good king who reigned from 750 until 731 B.C. Ahaz's son Hezekiah was a righteous man and he reigned from 715 until 686 B.C.

But you Bethlehem, David's country, the runt of the litter - from you will come the leader who will shepherd-rule Israel. He'll be no upstart, no pretender. His family tree is ancient and distinguished.

Micah 5:2 (MSG)

It is significant that Bethlehem, now known as the 'City of David,' was a very ordinary place and is only mentioned six times in the Old Testament prior to this prophecy. References can be found in Genesis 35:19, Judges 17:7, Ruth 1:1, Samuel 16:4; 2 Samuel 23:14 and Jeremiah

41:17. Matthew records this prophecy was fulfilled when Caesar Augustus imposed a census on the population.

> *After Jesus was born in Bethlehem in Judea, during the time of King Herod, Magi from the east came to Jerusalem and asked, "Where is the one who has been born King of the Jews? We saw his star when it rose and have come to worship him." When King Herod heard this he was disturbed, and all Jerusalem with him. When he had called together all the chief priests and teachers of the law, he asked them where the Messiah was to be born. "In Bethlehem in Judea," they replied, "for this is what the prophet has written: 'But you, Bethlehem, in the land of Judah, are by no means least among the rulers of Judah: for out of you will come a ruler who will shepherd my people Israel.'"*
>
> *Matthew 2:1-6 (NIV)*

In the third prophecy recorded in the book of Deuteronomy, Moses spoke to the Israelites and reminded them of God's commandments. This took place close to the River Jordan in the wilderness, shortly before they were about to enter the promised land. Unfortunately for Moses he had forfeited his right to enter the promised land due to his earlier disobedience.

Moses was born in Egypt and lived for 120 years until he died in Moab. According to the Encyclopedia of World Biography, Moses lived from 1392 until 1272 B.C.

> *"The LORD your God will raise up for you a prophet like me from among you, from your fellow Israelites. You must listen to him."*
>
> *Deuteronomy 18:15 (NIV)*

Luke records the fulfilment of this prophecy in the book of Acts, with an account of Peter preaching at a place called Solomon's Colonnade, where he proclaims that the coming prophet was none other than Jesus.

> *"Repent therefore, and turn to God so that your sins may be wiped out, so that times of refreshing may come from the presence of the Lord, and that he may send the Messiah appointed for you, that is Jesus ... Moses said, 'The Lord your God will raise up for you from your own people a prophet like*

me. You must listen to whatever he tells you. ... everyone who does not listen to that prophet will be utterly rooted out of the people.'"

Acts 3:19-23 (NRSV)

The fourth prophecy concerning the birth of Jesus Christ is the most well-known and is taken from the book of Isaiah.

For to us a child is born, to us a son is given, and the government will be on his shoulders and he will be called Wonderful Counsellor, Mighty God, Everlasting Father, Prince of Peace. Of the greatness of his government and peace there will be no end. He will reign on David's throne and over his kingdom, establishing it and upholding it with justice and righteousness from that time on and forever.

Isaiah 9:6-7 (NIV)

The fulfilment of this prophecy in the New Testament is recorded in Luke's Gospel.

"You will conceive and give birth to a son, and you are to call him Jesus. He will be great and will be called the Son of the Most High. The Lord God will give him the throne of his father David, and he will reign over Jacob's descendants for ever, his kingdom will never end."

Luke 1:31-33 (NIV)

The Unabridged Nativity Account

Although most commentators agree that out of the three synoptic Gospels Mark was written first, there is no agreement of when the books were written. Most scholars place the writers of Matthew and Luke around 70 A.D. but estimates vary between 50 and 90 A.D. The full account of the birth of Jesus Christ is contained in Matthew 1 and 2 and Luke 1 and 2. Both books complement each other, and when read in conjunction with each other, provide the full nativity account in its correct historical and chronological sequence. The following account is therefore a full sequential account of the birth of Jesus.

During the reign of King Herod there was a priest called Zechariah, who came from the priestly tribe of Abijah and was married to Elizabeth.

They were a very godly couple but had been unable to have any children because Elizabeth was infertile, and they were both now very elderly. One day Zechariah was carrying out his priestly duties, as it was the turn of his division to enter the tabernacle and burn incense. While the congregation were outside praying, he entered the inner part of the temple which only the priests were allowed to enter. Without warning the angel Gabriel appeared beside the altar and Zechariah was very afraid. The angel reassured him that his prayers for a child would be answered. Elizabeth would become pregnant and give birth to a son, whom they were to name John, and who would be filled with the Holy Spirit and proclaim the arrival of the Messiah. On hearing this, Zechariah was scornful and told the angel Gabriel that this was impossible because they were both very old. The angel insisted it was true, but because of Zechariah's disbelief, he told him he would be struck dumb until the day his son was born.

Whilst all this was going on, the congregation, who had been kept waiting a long time for Zechariah to reappear, became restless. When he eventually appeared, it was obvious to them he had seen a vision because he had been struck dumb and could only communicate using sign language.

Zechariah returned home and, as prophesied, Elizabeth his wife became pregnant. She was absolutely delighted and went off by herself for five months to enjoy her pregnancy.

When Elizabeth was six months pregnant, the angel Gabriel appeared to Mary in the village of Nazareth. Mary was quite shocked by the angel's appearance but was reassured and informed that God had a surprise for her. She was told she would become pregnant and give birth to a son, whom she was to call Jesus as he would be the promised Messiah. Mary wondered how she would become pregnant as she was still a virgin. The angel told her the Holy Spirit would make her pregnant; her child would be the Son of God. The angel also informed her Elizabeth her cousin was six months pregnant and that she was to remember nothing was impossible with God.

Mary believed the angel and immediately went straight to Zechariah's house and excitedly told Elizabeth everything that had happened. Elizabeth and Mary were both overjoyed and spontaneously burst out singing praises to God because they realized how privileged they were to be chosen by God for such an honour. Mary stayed with Elizabeth for the next three months and returned home to Joseph shortly before Elizabeth gave birth.

Once John had been born, all the relatives and neighbours celebrated his birth. On the eighth day, John was taken to the temple to be named and circumcised. The family wanted to name him Zechariah after his father, but Elizabeth disagreed and said he was to be named John. Zechariah was asked to give a definitive answer which he did by writing down that his name would be John. Zechariah had clearly learned his lesson! Zechariah was once again able to speak normally, and at once began praising and thanking God.

These events had a profound effect on everybody in the area, so much so that everybody talked about nothing else, particularly since Zechariah was filled with the Holy Spirit and was prophesying that John would become a prophet.

Although Mary was engaged to Joseph, they did not live together or have sexual relations but, just as the angel had promised, Mary discovered she was pregnant. When Joseph found out she was pregnant and he was not the father, he planned to discretely break off the engagement. However, an angel appeared to Joseph in a dream and told him to go ahead with their marriage plans because Mary was going to give birth to the Son of God who would be the Saviour of the world. They were told to name the baby Jesus.

Around the time Mary was due to give birth, Caesar Augustus ordered a census to take place throughout his Empire. This meant Mary and Joseph would have to travel from Nazareth in Galilee to Bethlehem in Judah where Joseph's family lived. This was a distance of about seventy miles, which would take them four to five days to complete, given Mary was heavily pregnant and due to give birth.

By the time Mary and Joseph had arrived in Bethlehem to give birth, all the accommodation had been filled and there were no vacancies in the hostel. In desperation they were allowed to be accommodated in the ground floor of the building, which was where the animals were kept at night when the temperature was cold. Once Mary had given birth there was no alternative but to wrap Jesus in any cloths that they could lay their hands on and they had no option but to place the baby Jesus in a manger. The Greek word *phatne* means a 'box' or 'crib' where animals feed.

At the same time, there were shepherds minding their own business, keeping watch over their sheep during the night, when suddenly without

Difficult Questions for Christians

warning an angel appeared to them lighting up the night sky – a sight that terrified them. After the angel had calmed them down they were told the great news that the Messiah had been born in Bethlehem. They were told to go and find the baby who would be lying in a manger, in a building used to house animals. While the shepherds were taking in this momentous news, a huge heavenly choir appeared and burst into song before returning back into heaven. The shepherds abandoned their sheep and ran to Bethlehem to see for themselves this miraculous revelation. On reaching Bethlehem everything was just as the angel had revealed and they told everybody what they had witnessed.

Eight days after Jesus was born, in accordance with Jewish law, Jesus was taken to the temple to be named and circumcised in a ceremony known as *brit milah* or *bris.*

Once Jesus was forty days old Mary and Joseph returned to the temple with Jesus to present him to the Lord and complete Mary's ritual purification following childbirth. They made a modest purification sacrifice comprising of two small birds, because they were so hard up they could not afford the customary lamb offering. Whilst in the temple they met a man called Simeon who was a Spirit-filled believer. The Holy Spirit had previously revealed to him that he would see the Messiah before he died. Prompted by the Holy Spirit, Simeon went into the temple, where he met Mary and Joseph. Simeon took Jesus in his arms, praised God and confirmed that Jesus was the Messiah, and prophesied that he would be the Saviour of the world, much to the surprise of Mary and Joseph. At the same time, they met a devoted prophetess called Anna, who was eighty-four years old and spent every waking moment in the temple. She also praised God and told everyone the good news about Jesus.

After their visit to Jerusalem was over they returned to Nazareth where Mary and Joseph managed to find suitable permanent accommodation in the town.

Events Two Years Later

When Jesus was approaching two years old, wise men from the East arrived in Nazareth bringing gifts for him. We are not told that there were three, but we do know that the Magi, which comes from Greek word *magos*, were very wealthy, well-educated astrologers, who came accompanied by their entourage of servants. Luke tells us they came from the East, an area we know today as Iran, Iraq, Saudi Arabia and the Yemen, and had been following a new star in the sky. After they arrived in Jerusalem they began asking around where the King of the Jews had been born.

When King Herod heard about this, he was very disturbed as he saw the Messiah as a potential rival. He called together all his high priests and teachers who advised him that the prophets had prophesied the coming Messiah would be born in Bethlehem. Herod sent the Magi on their way and told them to report back to him when they had found the child, so that he could go and worship this new king; but Herod planned to have his rival killed.

The wise men continued following the star until it stopped just where the family were living. When they entered the house and saw Jesus with his mother Mary, they worshipped him and handed over their gifts of gold, frankincense and myrrh; then they left. However, they were warned in a dream not to return to Herod, so they returned to their own country using a different route.

When Herod realized he had been tricked by the wise men, he was absolutely livid with rage and ordered his soldiers to go out and kill all children aged two years or under in and around Bethlehem. At the same time Joseph was warned by an angel in a dream to take Mary and Jesus and travel to Egypt as fast as possible, and to stay there until an angel appeared to them and told them it was safe to return. That same night they hurriedly departed for Egypt.

Following Herod's slaughter of all the children, there was a great outcry and a huge outpouring of grief, as had been prophesied by Jeremiah centuries earlier.

The Return of Jesus to Nazareth

Eventually, after King Herod died, an angel of the Lord appeared to Joseph and his family who were still in Egypt and told him it was safe for him to return to Israel with Mary and Jesus. When Joseph heard that Archelaus, Herod's son, had succeeded Herod as King of Judah, he was afraid to return.

After being warned in another dream the family made their way back to Nazareth, which Matthew records was fulfilment of another prophecy.

After these events we learn no more about Jesus, until he is twelve years old and returns to Jerusalem for the Feast of Passover, although his parents returned to Jerusalem every year to celebrate the Feast of the Passover.

A Personal Challenge

Christmas represents God's gift to the world 2,000 years ago of his son – Jesus!

> *For God so loved the world that he gave his only Son, that whoever believes in him shall not perish but have eternal life. For God did not send his son into the world to condemn the world, but to save the world through him.*
>
> *John 3:16-17 (NIV)*

Questions

Why was Jesus born in an insignificant place like Bethlehem?

_____

_____

What lessons can we learn from the appearance of the angels to Zechariah and Elizabeth?

_____

_____

Why do nativity plays portray the wise men visiting Jesus in a stable at Bethlehem?

_____

_____

How can we demonstrate 'goodwill to all men' at Christmas?

_____

_____

Should Christians celebrate Christmas given it was a pagan festival and does not represent the true birthday of Jesus?

_____

_____

What do we need to do to put 'Christ' back into Christmas?

_____

_____

POSTSCRIPT

How Can I Become a Christian?

STEP 1   Admit that you have sinned and need a Saviour to deal with your past and assure your future.

STEP 2   Believe that Jesus is the Son of God who died on the Cross to pay the penalty for your sins.

STEP 3   Receive Jesus as Saviour and Lord of your life by personal invitation and ask his forgiveness for your sins.

Why not pray this simple prayer now to invite Jesus into your life.

> *Heavenly Father, I confess that I have sinned and am separated from you. But I believe you showed your love for me by sending your Son Jesus to die on the Cross for my sins. So I turn to you, Lord Jesus, with great thankfulness. I surrender my life to you.*
>
> *I ask you to forgive me for all my sins, to cleanse me from all unrighteousness and to send the Holy Spirit to live in me as my friend, my teacher and my comforter.*
>
> *I reject Satan and every evil spirit in the name of Jesus Christ and I declare the Word of God, "If the Son has set you free, you are free indeed!" I declare that Jesus has set me free from all my sins and from every bondage of Satan.*
>
> *I have been born again, I am a child of God, I am a new creation, I have eternal life, in Jesus' mighty name. Amen.*[121]

---

[121] Reprinted from Voice magazine. Full Gospel Businessmen UK & Ireland. Used by permission © 2004.

Bibliography

A Time to Live – The Case Against Euthanasia and Assisted Suicide; George Pitcher

Angels; Billy Graham

Angels Elect and Evil; C. F. Dickason

Baptism: The Believer's First Obedience; Larry E. Dyer

Behaviour and Identity; David E. Jones

Brain, Consciousness and God, Daniel A. Helminiak

Dake's Annotated Reference Bible

The Encylopedia of World Biography

God's Truth about Gender: Unraveling the Lies of Modern Human Sexuality; David E. James IV

The Holy Spirit; Billy Graham

How to Live for Jesus; David Petts

Is There a Case for Assisted Dying? Paul Badham

Sexuality and Relationship Counselling; Tom Clinton

Shepherding in the Land; Hani Abu Damek

Unlocking the Bible Omnibus; David Pawson

Voice magazine; Full Gospel Businessmen UK & Ireland

Related Books from the Publisher

God Questions
Mike Hensman
ISBN 978-1-910197-51-6

In this helpful, easy-to-read guide, Rev. Mike Hensman tackles 46 of the most common questions concerning the Christian faith. With an endorsement from Nicky Gumbel, this is an excellent resource for anyone seeking answers to the important questions of life, as well as those who wish to grow further in their faith.

The Basics of Christianity
John-William Noble
ISBN 978-1-911086-16-1

What does it mean to be a Christian? Why do people get baptised? What is the point of church? John-William Noble answers these and other common questions about the Christian faith in this helpful interactive guide, useful for small groups or for individual study.

Available from your local Christian bookshop
or direct from the publisher:

www.onwardsandupwards.org